D0939001

BUILDING
THE CONTEST
ORATION

BUILDING
THE CONTEST
ORATION

BY

E. C. BUEHLER
Professor Emeritus of Speech
University of Kansas

AND

RICHARD L. JOHANNESEN
Instructor in Speech and Theatre
Indiana University

THE H. W. WILSON COMPANY
New York   *1965*

The Ideal Orator

In an orator, the acuteness of the logicians, the wisdom of the philosophers, the language almost of poetry, the memory of lawyers, the voice of tragedians, the gesture almost of the best actors, is required. Nothing therefore is more rarely found among mankind than a consummate orator.

—Cicero, *De Oratore*, 55 B.C.

Preface

This book is designed to meet the needs of the growing number of high school students who participate every year in some form of competitive educational oratory. Although there are many books on public speaking prepared for classroom purposes and a number of books on debate for both classroom and contest activities, little or nothing has been written in recent years to guide and assist the high school contest orator. Therefore this book is cast primarily in the form of a practical handbook; and it also contains information and observations which will help students appreciate the role of oratory in our culture and the place it has in competitive educational forensics.

Since so much of oratory is a thing of the human spirit, we have sought to develop overtones which would inspire young minds to engage in the ventures of contest oratory. We believe this kind of training helps the student to be not only a more able speaker but also a more responsible and mature citizen.

While the book is primarily directed to the student orator, it also aims to serve the high school speech teacher or the oratory "coach."

The book is simply organized, with the materials arranged in three parts. Part I is essentially an orientation section. It defines and explains the nature of oratory and gives a rationale for its existence. It deals with certain historical aspects of oratory and generally seeks to build positive attitudes toward competitive oratory. Part II is the heart of the book; it is devoted to the *complex* of procedures and processes for preparing and building the contest oration and delivering it in its completed form. Part III contains two college and five high school winning contest orations which are to be studied and which serve as sources of illustrative materials integrated in various ways with Part II. Furthermore, the seven orations are tersely analyzed and critically evaluated to reinforce and amplify the concepts discussed in Part II. The two appendixes dealing with building the extemporaneous speech and listing selected sources on the American Constitution, a prime subject of contest oratory, are further adjuncts of the book.

The authors are deeply grateful for ideas and insights drawn from hundreds of colleagues and hundreds of high school and college orators. Without these many close contacts with contest orators and their coaches for a combined total of nearly fifty years, this book could never have been written.

The junior author extends special acknowledgment to Professor Theodor LeVander of Augustana College, Rock Island, Illinois, for his patience, insight, and inspiration in teaching competitive oratory.

The authors express their appreciation to Mr. Bruno Jacob, Secretary of the National Forensic League, for his helpful suggestions, and gratefully acknowledge the assistance and permission of the following organizations in securing and using the selected winning contest orations in Part III: The American Legion, Future Farmers of America, Interstate Oratorical Association, Optimist International, and Veterans of Foreign Wars.

E. C. BUEHLER
RICHARD L. JOHANNESEN

Contents

BUILDING THE CONTEST ORATION

APPENDIXES

PART I

Getting a Perspective

CHAPTER 1

What Is Oratory?

Some words such as home, love, Americanism, education, and many others in common use have a variety of meanings, both abstract and concrete, which cannot be explicitly and completely defined in a few simple phrases or sentences. Oratory is such a word. It conveys various meanings to different people, and even these meanings are modified as changes occur in our culture.

Let's begin with the idea that oratory is a special kind of public speaking. The orator speaks for a special purpose, in a special way, at a special time. The idea that it is special or unique is important to keep in mind, for oratory is more than ordinary speech. The oration is a memorized, original, persuasive speech, dealing with worth-while subject matter of timely interest, demonstrating qualities of logic, organization, language, and delivery, and producing an effect of eloquence which is far above the ordinary. When we think of the classroom lecturer or the luncheon speaker, we normally do not expect oratory as such, even though such speakers may, at times, approach the oratorical. Oratory rises above the common level in its appeal and its emotional impact upon the listener. An oration is a creative effort by means of which important ideas are illuminated, emotionalized, ennobled, and dramatized. Its purpose is to impress, convince, or move the listener to action.

BUILDING THE CONTEST ORATION

Aristotle defined oratory as "the faculty of finding all the means of persuasion on a subject." Quintilian, the Roman rhetorician often considered the greatest speech teacher of all time, viewed it as "the art of speaking well," and Cicero considered it as "the art of persuasion." These classical definitions of oratory, in their essentials, remain with us today. Max Eastman, a contemporary literary critic, says, "Oratory at its best is a dramatic art. It is the art of speaking lines you have written and acting the part of yourself." T. V. Smith, late professor of philosophy at the University of Chicago, reminded us that prose is useful to make things clear, poetry is useful to make things appreciated, but oratory serves to get things done. He pointed out that prose is the servant of the scientist, poetry is the servant of the lover, while oratory is the servant of the statesman. Oratory, then, remains the highest form of communication, useful in tapping those resources in an audience which represent the better side of human nature.

The Greeks, who were known for their idealism, looked upon oratory as among the noblest of all arts, and to them the oration was the aristocrat of all forms of public speaking. The orator, among the ancient Greeks and Romans, was looked upon with high esteem. He was highly respected and greatly admired and was considered a citizen of unusual ability and influence.

In a sense, an oration is your best speech, dressed up in your best language, with the better part of your nature wrapped up in it. It is important to think of an oration as being more than a mere photographed picture

16

of thought and feeling. It gives the audience more than a snapshot view of an idea as a candid camera would. An oration is a portrait of a compelling thought. It must go far beyond mere facts and details. It speaks to the listener's soul and conscience, appeals to his aesthetic sense.

Briefly, then, oratory is commonly characterized by formality and dignity, by the speaker's originality and his high intent, by soundness of reason, and by the generous use of language which is rich in imagery. Words are memorized and the speaker's total self and personality are genuinely involved in the entire speaking process. The word "oratory" refers to the artful process of the speaking performance; the word "orator" refers to the author, the originator, and the manipulator of the speaking process. He is also called the "speaker." The word "oration" means the composed speech in its final rhetorical form. It is also called the "speech."

Thus we see that oratory, like any art, may be explained and defined from many points of view. In formulating these definitions, we should take into consideration the individuality of the orator himself. Since persons in oratory differ, perhaps no definition of oratory can be categorically devised to stand all the tests of criticism which may arise. This situation, however, should not cause us to be discouraged. On the contrary, this situation gives us cause to rejoice, for the goals of oratory, which are to impress or persuade, remain clear and constant. We should be glad for the fact that the means of attaining these goals give the orator great freedom in the way he may exercise and apply his creative mind and draw upon his own personal resources and thus apply his creative ability as he wishes.

It should be clear now to the reader that an oration is not, as some students seem to think, a "glorified" extemporaneous speech. Neither is it an artificial, insincere, emotional, flamboyant display of high-sounding words and phrases. (Unfortunately, for some people the image of oratory is exactly that.) An oration is not, in essence, a speech to inform, although it may contain much information; it is not a speech to entertain, although it may have some qualities of entertainment; it is not just a debate, although it *must* contain sound argument. Neither is it a prize essay orally rendered like a dramatic declamation, even though, like an essay, it should demonstrate unity, coherence, balance, and clarity.

CHAPTER 2

Our Rich Heritage in Oratory

Oral communication of various types and forms underlies the cultures of people and their civilizations, both past and present. Man has forever shaped his destiny with his tongue. But most spoken words, like autumn leaves, fall with only fleeting notice. Only the slightest trickle of the vast oceans of output lodges permanently in print and becomes available to us as speech literature. Only part of this literature may be classified as oratory by speech critics. The orator speaks for a special purpose in a special way at a specific time. Even though we could devote years to the study and reading of what has been written about great orators, their orations, and their methods, we would cover only a tiny speck of the total literature, so vast is our heritage of oratorical and rhetorical works.

ANCIENT GREECE

Obviously, we owe much to the Greeks and Romans. Rhetoric, the formal theory of the practice of oratory, played an important role in secondary education in Athens as early as 600 B.C. One famous teacher, Isocrates, a pupil of Socrates, had a private school of oratory in which he taught for nearly fifty years, and his pupils often spent three or four years in rounding out their studies. The oratorical training in Isocrates' school was practical. He prepared his students for life

and its problems. His was no school of learning which promised to make full-fledged orators in ten easy lessons. He educated the mind and the character of his pupils for service to the nation. His ideal was the orator-statesman.

The Greek philosopher Aristotle was deeply interested in rhetoric and oratory, and his writings have made a great impact upon speech educators through the centuries. In the prime of his intellectual life he wrote his *Rhetoric*, which outlined the sound persuasive principles underlying oratory.

Demosthenes stood as a tower of strength, not only as an orator but as a statesman and by example a teacher of oratory. Since he is considered by some to be the greatest orator of all times, let us become better acquainted with him as a person and as a master of eloquence. The safety and welfare of Athens was always primary in his mind. He effectively employed the power of his oratory to warn Athens of threats by enemies from without and within.

An extensive body of largely authentic lore has come down to us concerning Demosthenes' self-training in oratory. As a young man he showed little promise of oratorical greatness. He was shy, awkward in bodily movement, physically weak, and afflicted with enunciation defects. But Demosthenes was determined to possess the power of eloquence. To build up his body and overcome shortness of breath, he constantly ran long distances. Also, he developed vocal force by going to the seashore and attempting to outshout the waves while practicing an oration. Demosthenes realized that concentration and dedication were necessary for his improvement. Hence, he secluded himself in a cave or underground room. Here he practiced his vocal and physical delivery in front of a mirror. To avoid the temptation of leaving the cave before his task of self-improvement was complete, he shaved half of his head bald; the potential ridicule of society kept him at work. He overcame his enunciation problems by speaking with pebbles in his mouth; the resulting exaggerated articulation helped to smooth out his enunciation defects. Demosthenes was also afflicted with a nervous twitch or upward jerking of one shoulder when speaking. To overcome this problem, he suspended just above his shoulder a razor-sharp sword which forced him to keep the shoulder steady while practicing. Certainly everyone cannot become a Demosthenes, but his efforts do demonstrate that a person who is dedicated to self-improvement in oratory can overcome drawbacks and become a competent public speaker.

ANCIENT ROME

Oratory, more than any other study, also occupied the attention of the talented Roman youth. The Romans, being of a practical turn of mind, viewed oratory as a necessary tool in politics, law, and all civic and public affairs. Young men planning to go into law or politics took oratorical training as a prerequisite to their profession. Here, in a sense, we have a hint of our modern practice of making a basic speech course a requirement for college graduation.

BUILDING THE CONTEST ORATION

Oratory among the Romans was considered the highest of callings, and it was studied seriously and extensively. Quintilian was the most famous oratorical teacher in Rome. He was born about the time of Jesus' death. He strove to build the perfect orator, "a good man skilled in speaking." He did not believe a person was born with the gift of oratory but admitted that a natural aptitude would be helpful in developing oratorical eloquence. He believed that you could not divorce a man's character from his speaking performance. He put great stress upon the speaker's use of his own individuality and insisted that each orator must develop his oratorical powers in his own way. Thus, in the eyes of Quintilian, Cato stood out as a rugged man possessing great mental ability, whereas Caesar was noted for his vigor, Cassius for his severity, and Brutus for his gravity. Quintilian considered Cicero as one approaching the ideal orator, for he seemed to possess all of the attributes which an orator needs.

On the horizon of Roman oratory, Cicero even today is a towering figure. He was a statesman, an orator, and a rhetorician who sincerely admired Demosthenes. His youth was an austere one, and it might be said that he was a country boy who grew up under great hardships and made good in the big city. He renounced the common pleasures of life such as parties and sports and rigidly disciplined himself to the challenge of becoming a great orator. Like Demosthenes, he was willing to pay the price for his success. He made a great many speeches and was one of the most outstanding orators of all time. He was a fierce competitor in the courts of law and sometimes compromised ethical standards to win a case at all costs. But his faults were minor compared to his real ability as an orator and his reputation as a good man. Great as was his contribution as a practicing orator, probably his most valuable contribution for us who are interested in the cause of oratory comes from the works he wrote about it. This is a rich heritage for which modern students should be eternally grateful.

What are some of the lessons we can learn from Cicero and his oratory? He taught us the value of perseverance and industry. He worked at his art constantly and never gave up. He taught us the importance of good speech composition. His oratory was founded upon the scientific principles of rhetoric. He taught us that the speaker must have sound ideas and that his arguments must hold water. His speeches were carefully structured on the basis of sound evidence and logic. He taught us the importance of clarity and audience interest. He made copious use of illustration, utilized the emotion of his listeners, usually spoke upon subjects pertaining to human dignity, and appealed to the higher feelings of his listeners. He taught us the importance of the speaker's "ethos" or reputation. Although he was human and not without fault, he maintained the image of a good man, trusted, respected, and liked by his audiences. All in all, his speeches were in keeping with the central picture of what is good oratory: convincing men through logic, moving them by emotional appeals, speaking as one having the authority of an ethical, responsible, mature person.

Cicero marks the pinnacle of Roman oratory. With the advent of the Roman Empire and the loss of full political liberty, the art declined, just as it did in Greece after the coming of Alexander the Great.

Following the glories of Greece and Rome came a thousand years during which rhetoric and oratory passed through what was virtually a dark age. During medieval times, what little interest was shown in oratory was mild and sporadic and occurred primarily in the area of preaching.

ENGLAND

There were signs of an awakening of interest in speaking activities in England at the beginning of the fifteenth century. In a limited way, attention was given to speaking exercises in both the grammar schools and the established universities. In the sixteenth, seventeenth, and eighteenth centuries debates, declamations, and original oratory enjoyed a reasonable degree of popularity at school festivals, assemblies, farewell occasions, and commencements. Emphasis was placed upon articulation and pronunciation in the grammar schools and more attention given to thought and composition at the university level. Of course, throughout the eighteenth and nineteenth centuries, such noted English orators as Lord Chatham, Edmund Burke, Charles James Fox, Richard Sheridan, William Pitt the Younger, and William Ewart Gladstone were matured in the fires of debate in Parliament.

In general, the elocution movement, which overemphasized the study of vocal and physical delivery, was making itself felt throughout England and her schools between 1750 and 1850. This influence, to a degree, reached across the Atlantic but really did not take hold on our shores to a great extent until after the Civil War. We now turn to oratory in the United States.

THE UNITED STATES

Oratory and other forms of public speaking played a vital role in the growth and development of our country. No nation of prominence in the history of civilization has shaped so much of its own destiny by oratory. Perhaps no nation during the last two centuries has produced so much in the way of oratorical materials worthy of publication and study. Certainly no country during the past fifty years has experienced so much growth and expansion in speech education.

In our over-all historical picture of American oratory we will view simultaneously educational oratory and oratory of the public platform. The two are interrelated and intertwined as was the case with the ancient Greeks and Romans. Before we take a closer look at some of our outstanding oratorical figures and before we examine the role of educational oratory, we should give some thought to the underlying conditions within our culture which helped bring oratory and speech education into prominence.

First of all, we must keep in mind that we were and still are a new nation, growing up, in a relative sense, in a revolutionary environment. We are children of the spirit of revolt, revolt against tyranny and autocratic rule. Our founding fathers set out, bravely and whole-heartedly, on a venture for national independence and individual freedom. The words "liberty or death" have been on the lips of every schoolboy since the Declaration of Independence. We inherited a fire and zeal for the noble experiment in human dignity, and we fell heir to a brand new set of laws dealing with human rights. Our ideals of liberty and freedom were further enhanced by our living in a land of promise, a new land of vast opportunities for an abundant life. Jefferson's phrase, "the pursuit of happiness," had unusual meaning as the open spaces and vast resources of the continent lay before the eyes of our forefathers.

The Constitution itself was an inspiration for oratory. This very instrument was a product of the spoken word. This law of the land was hammered out over the long hot summer months of 1787 by discussion and debate. The makers of the Constitution believed that in order to make freedom and democracy live the people must have the right to talk openly and freely at all times about their problems. Freedom of speech is the life-blood of democratic government, and basic in their formula for a democratic nation were the provisions for freedom of speech and assembly, precious rights for a free-minded people. Naturally, oratory flourished among men who earnestly sought to make democracy work. The Constitution gave the "go" sign to freedom of speech; thus, everywhere, laws were fashioned on the anvil of debate in town councils, state legislatures, and the halls of Congress. The town-hall meeting became a common institution. Oratory helped to settle disputes and elect men to office. The young nation grew rapidly, establishing new territories and admitting new states to the Union. A crisis which was to culminate in a great tragedy soon was in the making, with its vast political, social, and moral consequences. The crucial issues of states' rights, followed by and enmeshed in the issue of slavery, were not to be resolved by oratory but by civil war. Even now, we bear the scars of this war, a war leaving in its aftermath the great issues of civil rights and integration. Yet this war and the issues involved before and after the conflict brought forth some of our finest oratory from a decade or two before the first shot was fired at Fort Sumter to a half century or more after Lee's surrender.

Oratory is often at its best when born in the fires of crisis, fear, turmoil, and human suffering. The orator must have a cause to which he gives great moral earnestness. Thus, out of wars, hard times, and the pains of our national growth comes most of our oratorical heritage.

It is difficult to think of our Revolutionary and Constitutional fathers without thinking of such orators as Patrick Henry, Benjamin Franklin, Alexander Hamilton, George Washington, Thomas Jefferson, James Madison. It is difficult to think of pre-Civil War developments, the conflict itself, and its aftermath without thinking of John C. Calhoun, Henry Clay, Daniel Webster, John Quincy Adams, Abraham Lincoln, Stephen A. Douglas, Henry Ward Beecher, Henry Grady, Robert Ingersoll, Wendell Phillips and many others. It is difficult to think of World War I without

BUILDING THE CONTEST ORATION

Woodrow Wilson, Robert La Follette, Sr., Henry Cabot Lodge, and William Borah; of the great depression of the thirties without thinking of Franklin D. Roosevelt and his fireside chats; or of World War II without Presidents Roosevelt and Truman.

AMERICAN EDUCATIONAL ORATORY

The development of educational oratory is almost unique in America. During the first decade of its existence, Harvard insisted upon oratorical practice among its students. Orations were given in Latin and Greek, as well as English. From 1642 to 1700, orations were featured at commencements. Princeton gave heavy emphasis to oratory; other colonial colleges stressing oratory included Amherst, William and Mary, and Dartmouth. By the time of the Civil War, wide acclaim was given to oratory as an extracurricular activity; when it took that form, it was largely controlled and promoted by college literary societies.

It is interesting to note that oratory was so highly regarded at Harvard that from 1806 to 1809 United States Senator John Quincy Adams, later President of the United States, held the Boylston Professorship of Rhetoric and Oratory. He lectured and presided over students' orations. In 1810 his *Lectures on Rhetoric and Oratory* were published.

Oratorical training continued through the Civil War period and beyond. The school orator stood out as a potent campus figure, but he had to share his glory with other exponents of literary talent, the poet, essayist, and college magazine editor. Intercollegiate competitive oratory in the United States came on the scene at Knox College, Galesburg, Illinois, February 11, 1873. The colleges represented were Monmouth, Abingdon, Lombard, and Knox. Out of this beginning, the Interstate Oratorical Association was formed the following year. This organization, probably the oldest of its kind in America, held its first contest February 27, 1874. The colleges participating in this historic event were Iowa College, Grinnell; Monmouth College, Monmouth, Illinois; Chicago University; Iowa State University, Iowa City; Beloit College, Beloit, Wisconsin; Illinois State Industrial University, Champaign.

Soon other intercollegiate leagues came into being and flourished. The college orator was a highly honored and glamorized figure, perhaps even surpassing that campus idol of today, the star fullback of the winning team. So popular were the oratorical contests that it was not uncommon for railroads to run special trains to the site of the event, and school victories were celebrated with bonfires, blaring bands, and student parades. In some instances, ten per cent of the student body tried out for an oratorical contest. Oratory was the forerunner of another popular activity, intercollegiate debating, by about two decades.

Some of our greatest American orators received valuable early training in oratory in their literary societies or in intercollegiate contests. Daniel Webster was a college orator at Dartmouth. Others receiving oratorical experience in college literary societies were Rufus Choate, Henry Ward Beecher, Henry Grady, Albert Beveridge, Booker T. Washington, and Woodrow Wilson. Robert La Follette, Sr., won first place in the interstate contest in 1879, and William Jennings Bryan participated in oratorical events in a literary society at Illinois College. Senator Wayne Morse and Harold E. Stassen were competitors in the Northern Oratorical League.

Oratory in the high schools prevailed in the late 1800's. It was stressed in both curricular and extracurricular activities, and was frequently taught in "declamation" courses, which emphasized memorized recitation of famous speeches. In the early decades of the present century, speech courses began to be taught in the United States and gained wide acceptance. These new courses stressed creation of original content and organization as well as techniques of delivery. By 1920, speech in the high school curriculum had become more common.

After World War I, there was a strong emphasis on high school interscholastic oratory on the subject of the Constitution and its founders. From 1924 to the mid-1930's, the high school National Oratorical Contest on the Constitution was sponsored by over fifty leading American newspapers, including the New York *Times*. By 1926 this contest was international in scope. The seven or eight national finalists were judged in Washington by the chief justice and four associate justices of the Supreme Court. President Calvin Coolidge presided at the 1926 international final contest. Attractive prizes included a championship cup for the national winner and a two-and-a-half-month summer tour of Europe for the national finalists. Since 1938 a somewhat similar contest emphasizing the Constitution has been sponsored by the American Legion, now with some 350,000 participants annually. The Optimist International has sponsored a national oratory contest since 1928. The Voice of Democracy contest, originated by the National Association of Broadcasters in 1947, now is sponsored by the Veterans of Foreign Wars; over 200,000 high school students participate annually. The Future Farmers of America long have sponsored contests in oratory. Many 4-H clubs at the local level, some metropolitan newspapers, and over thirty state activities associations have encouraged competitive speaking at the high school level. Competitive oratory is also sponsored by the Knights of Pythias, Lions Club, and Native Sons of the Golden West. The National Forensic League, founded in 1925, has supported and encouraged high school interscholastic oratory from its beginning through a system of honors and awards. Each year it sponsors a national speech tournament in which the participants are over thirty orators who have won first place in their state association or National Forensic League contests. Another sixty high-ranking speakers who have elected oratory as their second event engage in competition with the regular winners of state and NFL contests. Thus the total number of high school students now participating in contest oratory well exceeds half a million a year.

CHAPTER 3

You and Contest Oratory

A Venture in Self-Improvement

First of all, it is well to look upon contest oratory as a learning experience. It is a special form of training in speech communication. Obviously, many of the noted orators of whom we have spoken in glowing terms may not provide examples suited to your own needs. However, you can learn much from studying these men and their methods and observing their attitudes toward oratory. The great masters, in a sense, stand as ideals rather than as models to be imitated.

Perhaps it is reassuring to remember that in their youth Demosthenes, Cicero, Patrick Henry, Abraham Lincoln, Daniel Webster, Winston Churchill, and a host of others gave little promise of ever becoming able orators. In fact, some of these men suffered from speech impediments, excessive stage fright, severe awkwardness or shyness, and, in fact, probably seemed destined to be oratorical failures. Perhaps most students who read these lines show neither more nor less promise of becoming competent orators than the men we have mentioned. At this stage in your development, no one can tell what hidden powers for effective oral communication lie dormant in you. The road to good oratory is long and fraught with incidents of failure and periods of discouragement, but the ultimate rewards are immeasurable.

32

YOU AND CONTEST ORATORY

Make the slogan "A quitter never wins and a winner never quits" your own, and you have taken the first important step. It isn't so much whether you win or lose that counts, but, as the old saying goes, how you play the game, and not once but again and again. It is the training, the experience, and your personal growth that mean most to you. Look upon the oratorical contest as a valuable opportunity for self-improvement.

REWARDS AND SATISFACTIONS

What are some of the probable rewards and satisfactions that grow out of such experiences? It might be interesting for you to make your own inventory. But here is one inventory offered by a young student orator, slightly rephrased for our purpose here. Perhaps you may have a better inventory.

1. The oration helped me to do some original thinking of my own. I could feel myself growing in self-reliance.

2. I learned a lot about a definite subject. It was richly rewarding for me to get a wealth of information and a new perspective on a vital issue.

3. I found that writing an oration was excellent training in English composition. It taught me to make a better choice of words and to express my ideas more clearly, more accurately, and with greater brevity. It gave me an appreciation of the power of language and how it can be used to adorn and glorify an idea. It was exciting at times when I could dream up an effective figure of speech or an unusually colorful phrase. I learned a lot about

33

putting ideas together to make a complete and unified thought picture. In fact, I sometimes feel that I got more real help in matters of English composition than I did in the regular English course.

4. After the contest was over, there came that great moment when I knew that I had done it. I made that speech before an audience and before judges, and I knew I was part of the show. It was an experience in which I felt I was doing something important for myself and my school. It was worth more than money can buy.

5. I learned how to improve my speech delivery. Since I had to rehearse my oration many times, I could give more attention to precision in articulating words, and I learned the meaning of the term "beauty of diction." I also learned to develop a sense of rhythm and how to deal with dramatic emphasis. In an oration you are, in a sense, acting a part, something you do not do in most other speeches, and this sort of training is only possible through frequent rehearsals.

6. Perhaps most of all, the experience of being in that contest gave me a new feeling of self-respect and a feeling of self-discovery. This inner satisfaction makes it easier for me to live with myself and feel more at ease among my classmates, friends, and teachers.

MAKING UP YOUR MIND

To enter or not to enter, that is the question. Of course, there may be times when you really don't have much choice. You may be enlisted or drafted by your teacher. However, if you find yourself pushed into a contest somewhat against your will, you still can reappraise your thinking to make your entry as if it were your own choice. The right mental attitude and the proper spirit are something you need to develop by yourself. Make it your business not to be the "reluctant dragon." If you do a good job developing a positive attitude toward making and delivering the oration, the chances are that you will be as well off as the fellow who made the choice of his own free will, perhaps haphazardly, many, many months ago, or even better off than he. You at least will not be stuck with a desire which has been with you too long and gone stale, or a desire which was partly artificial and synthetic in the first place. You have a fresh, newly created desire, and, don't forget, if the teacher has singled you out to represent your school in oratory, you are someone special. This is a sign that others have confidence in you, and if others believe in you, you have cause to believe in yourself.

On Being Sensible About It

Why Fret and Worry?

The fact that you are going to engage in a competitive event may at first cause you some worry and feelings of apprehension. Perhaps just the thought of getting up to speak before an audience or judge may be a bit frightening. But if stage fright alone is your bugaboo, you really have no cause to worry. This is natural and there is nothing unusual about it. This shows you are just like anyone else.

The able and experienced orator Cicero counsels us wisely on this point. In his book *De Oratore,* Cicero confesses: "So in my own case I constantly experience this feeling; I turn pale at the beginning of a speech, my brain whirls, and I tremble in every limb." Cicero realized, however, that well-controlled nervous tension was natural and essential: "I have observed that . . . first rate speakers . . . are somewhat uneasy at the beginning of a speech . . . , that the more able a speaker was, the more nervous he was. . . . For the better the speaker the more painfully is he conscious of the difficulty of speaking."

Truthfully, this feeling of speech fright is a good sign; it shows you have a sense of pride and that you care about what others think about you and your speech. You start off with a built-in dynamo enabling you to do your best. Furthermore, it is more of a feeling of excitement than anything else, similar to that experienced by an actor just before the curtain rises or the baseball pitcher or football quarterback at the start of the crucial game. In reality, this feeling is a blessing, not a curse. Welcome it and you will soon learn to live with it and make it work for you.

Don't Be Afraid of Competition

Perhaps you hate the thought of competition, and this is in itself part of the cause of your anxiety. But doesn't this seem silly when you think of the fact that almost everything you do in school, be it in class, on the athletic field, or at a party, involves competition? You compete for grades in school, for points or scores in games, and for status or recognition at social events. Competition of one form or another is an inescapable factor in life.

As we look more closely at this matter of competition, we come face to face with the role of self-determination. You will probably be in the company of the more gifted and able students in school. As you reflect upon this high level of competition, you may be tempted at first to think how good other contestants will be compared to yourself. This is starting off on the wrong track. If you start off fretting about the other person only in terms of comparing his anticipated performance with yours, you will generate more self-consciousness. Don't worry about the other fellow. You can't do much about that anyway. You have only one chief competitor —yourself. You can do something about that. Make it your absorbing ambition not to sell yourself short. Start right off by exploring your many personal resources. Dig down into your deeper and inmost self to awaken talents which you yourself perhaps have been hiding. Get yourself totally involved and put your whole mind to work. Surrender your total self to the challenge and don't be afraid to surprise even yourself with what you can do. This all-out effort of self-determination to draw upon your reserve powers will make a big difference in this type of competition. In other words, go all out to develop your oration in your own way according to your best ability. Be always concerned about how to do your best and forget about what others may do.

Don't Be a Copy Cat

Don't be a copy cat. Put the stamp of *you* all over your oration. Keep in mind that this is *your* speech, not your coach's or your school's. Make it yours all the way. The prime source of eloquence lies in your sincerity, your purpose, your desire, your enthusiasm, your creative ideas, and your total self. Build the image in the mind of your listeners that you speak as one having authority.

Plagiarism, the use of someone else's words or ideas as your own without crediting the source, is viewed as the unpardonable sin of the contest orator, just as it is of any other speaker or writer. Although a student guilty of plagiarism may not risk a prison sentence, the stigma of dishonesty and betrayal of faith upon the offender and his school is such that it rivals many types of crime. Any contestant flagrantly guilty of plagiarism faces the penalty of being disqualified from a contest, of forfeiting awards or money dishonorably won. What is still worse, others may suffer as well, for the plagiarist's school may be forced to forfeit its right to participate in further interscholastic speech contests for a period of time. The consequences of plagiarism are thus severe for both the orator and his school. Bruno E. Jacob, secretary and founder of the National Forensic League, which annually sponsors high school speech tournaments, reports that his greatest source of trouble is the problem of plagiarism.

Yourself and Your Goals in Review

Oratory is at its best when the orator can strike a happy balance in the use of sound logic and emotional appeals. Facts and logic alone are somewhat cold and impotent. Emotion by itself without evidence can leave the audience without a sense of purpose or even create feelings of frustration and general embarrassment. The oration must not be top-heavy with either logic or emotion. The listener should be prompted to think and stimulated to feel at the same time. Sound sense shot through with sincere feeling helps to create understanding and arouse the will to action.

There is no simple all-purpose formula for preparing an oration, no simple, easy-to-follow set of directions such as one might find in a recipe for baking a cake. Here again Cicero gives wise counsel as he outlines the qualifications for his "ideal" orator in *De Oratore:*

> In an orator, the acuteness of the logicians, the wisdom of the philosophers, the language almost of poetry, the memory of lawyers, the voice of tragedians, the gesture almost of the best actors, is required.

An oration should somehow, at some time, grip the listener and leave him "shook up." You must strike a blow, as it were, to the listener's solar plexis. The prize fighter often scores his victory with one single knock-out punch. Baseball games are often won with one single stroke of the bat. The orator, likewise, must be able to deliver that extra punch; he must have some high point with a communication impact that penetrates into the listener's conscience.

It is clear that the creation and delivery of the oration are an individualistic undertaking, something each speaker must work out for himself. Nevertheless, he should start with some knowledge of the basic principles involved. Hence Part II of this book is designed by the authors as a guide for preparing and delivering an oration, and it develops in detail many essential theories and principles which underly the total process. We believe the student of oratory will find this helpful.

Part III comprises seven samples of winning contest orations and accompanying analyses based upon the principles discussed in Part II.

PART II

Getting to Work

CHAPTER 4

Steps in Preparing the Oration

The actual methods of preparing an oration will naturally vary from speaker to speaker. Methods will be influenced by your general knowledge of the subject, the resource material available, your desire to attain excellence of performance, your aptitude for creative thinking, the specific purpose of your speech, and the counsel you may get from your coach, your teachers, and others. Preparation must always be governed to a degree by individual traits, the rules of the contest, and the conditions under which the contest is held.

We present six steps in the preparation of an oration which usually follow in sequence. The steps are not completely separate. They tend to overlap each other and are integrated. For example, step one is not to be achieved and then forgotten, but should be carried over into all the remaining steps. Steps five and six concerning memorization and delivery complement each other and may, to a large degree, be integrated. Of course the material presented in Chapters 5-8 is to be applied during these six steps.

1. *Develop the proper frame of mind.* An oration is a creative piece of writing and requires imaginative thinking. It must reflect ideas, attitudes, and feelings which originate in your mind and belong to you. It is a speech of your invention and must grow out of your desire to speak forth on an important matter in a compelling and orderly manner. Your sense of excitement will help you to prepare and deliver a better oration

than you would if you approached the task as something dull and uninteresting.

A proper mood or desire is something that has to be developed. It may not come at once. It is not something you can turn on or off like a water faucet. There is no magic formula for creating the proper spirit as you get ready for the contest. We can only make a few suggestions in the hope that some will be of use to you. First, you will need time to be alone. Even football players before a crucial game need mental preparation for their best efforts. Get off by yourself so that you may ponder and contemplate the kind of speech you would like to make. Talk to yourself silently or audibly. Perhaps "philosophize" aloud. You are trying to get yourself in tune in order that your mind may function more harmoniously. Enthusiasm may be slow in coming to you, but here patience and effort will be rewarding. Extend this humble beginning in the form of mental doodling, scribbling notes, writing a single point in paragraph form, dreaming up new figures of speech to make points clear or impressive. You can help yourself further by reading a few chapters of a book, or some magazine articles dealing with your subject. Sometimes you can get help by listening to a speech, by talking to a friend or teacher. But make up your mind that you really want to enter an oratorical contest, not only for personal glory but for your personal development. Think of the contest as an opportunity which may never come again. Don't expect a burst of inspiration to come to you out of the blue by simply sitting around and twiddling your thumbs. Apples won't fall into your lap just because you sit idly under the apple tree. You will need to rustle about, shake some branches, or climb the tree before you can enjoy the fruit. Thus effort is the first step toward developing a suitable frame of mind. Get yourself involved, think, read, write, discuss. "Doing" generates the initial inspiration which will set off a chain reaction to help you lose yourself in what you are doing. When this happens, you have found the proper spirit.

2. *Determine your objective and find a suitable topic.* Although your speech belongs to the persuasive type, you should decide in your mind specifically what your central purpose should be and what you want to emphasize in your speech. Get your object well in mind and it will be easier to select and line up your subject matter.

The orator seeks some type of verdict from his listeners. He may be primarily concerned with proving something to be true or false—for example, that a problem exists—relying mainly on facts and logic. He may be concerned with firing his listeners to a high pitch of enthusiasm about some ideal or principle in which they already believe. In this case, his goal is to impress his listeners. Or he may be concerned with motivating listeners to take some form of action, in which case he must not only prove that a problem exists, but also put forward a sound solution. Or he may seek a combination of two or more such verdicts. It is important, therefore, to settle on the type of verdict which you want most; this will influence the manner and method of both preparation and delivery.

Although your general subject area may be designated by the American Legion, the Optimist International, the Future Farmers of America, or other groups, you will still have the problem of pinpointing or narrowing your topic to more specific subject matter. Many factors should be considered in selecting your topic, but don't expect to find a perfect topic. It is important to select a subject area and a specific part of it which appeals to you. The subject should be timely and of wide public interest. It should not be too broad nor too narrow. You should seek a subject which contains specific factual matter and about which there is sufficient available library material. Try to select a subject about which you can say something new or one which you can treat in an unusual, interesting, and original manner. Triteness is a difficult obstacle to overcome. Aim first at having something vital, worth-while, and insightful to say and only second at winning through doing your very best.

3. *Think—read—explore.* This is usually the key step, determining whether you win or lose. It is well to start off with what you already know and what you can dream up on your own. Stimulate your mind with the help of related reading matter within your immediate reach. Get a quick preview of the subject area. More serious and extensive reading will come later. Just now you are feeling your way. Comb your mind for all kinds of ideas and possible approaches. Have many private "brain-storming" sessions when you jot down almost anything that occurs to you as bearing on the subject. Don't worry at this time about testing or evaluating everything you think of. This is the germination

period in the process of creative thinking. Ideas thus germinated may be cultivated and developed more fully later. Discuss some of these points with your teachers, your coach, friends, classmates, members of the family, or any other intelligent person who may lend a sympathetic ear. It is well to keep note paper handy so that you may jot down diary notes to yourself. Capture the bursts of light and inspiration where and when they occur.

Having thought yourself empty, so to speak, and having pretty well exhausted your preliminary resources of reading and talks with others, you are ready to read yourself full and soak up vast amounts of facts, expert opinion and value judgments in books, magazines, and pamphlets. The sound contest oration, like the sound debate case, is based on intensive, extensive, and objective research on the topic. Cicero stressed in his *De Oratore* that the true virtue of oratory "cannot have full play unless the speaker has mastered the subject on which he intends to speak." Read with an open mind. Seek to grasp ideas clearly, deepen your insights and gain a broad perspective on your subject. Teachers and librarians should help direct you to the most pertinent reading matter. Quality of reading matter is more important than quantity. Often one or two outstanding works on the Constitution, for example, which are carefully read and digested will prove more helpful than a long list of mediocre books. Seek source material that is reliable and largely objective. Don't worry about repetitious material. This can help to firm up concepts in your mind. Once you have a firm grasp of your subject, all other aspects of the process such as organization, writing, memorization, and delivery will be much easier and more readily mastered. Furthermore, the final, specific position on a subject taken by you in your oration should emerge only *after* completion of all research.

4. *Formulate the speech and write.* Now that you have read yourself full and have a perspective on your subject, you are ready to give shape and order to your materials. There are many ways this may be done. A common practice is to develop a long, detailed outline before writing the first line. This plan, however, may be better suited for developing a debate speech than an oration. We feel this plan, if rigidly carried out, may lead to a speech in which the quality of writing may suffer because the speech is overstructured, stiff, rigid, and inflexible. In an oration the thought and purpose should govern the overall design and structure. A fixed outline and structure should not govern the central idea and purpose of the oration. Writing and organizational factors can be effectively integrated. Thus the two dimensions of language and organization can be developed concurrently and be integrated.

Before you start writing your speech, it is important that you are full of your subject, so full, in fact, that you feel you have reached a bursting point and you must express yourself in some way. In order to have unity and compactness in substance, it is well to start off by stating your central thesis in a single sentence of twenty-five words. See how much meaning you can pack into this sentence. You may make numerous trial runs in formulating this statement. It may be necessary to do this eight or ten times before you reach a level which satisfies you. After you have done this, the next step is to draft a statement of not more than 150 words giving a condensed abstract of your message. These two steps, when carefully carried out, will discipline your mind to stay with your central idea and develop a sense of unity. Now you are ready to make a rough outline of the essential points of your speech. This should be done fairly rapidly without filling in all the details. With a sketchy outline in mind, you are ready to put on paper a rough and perhaps awkward word picture of your oration.

If possible, you should try to write the entire speech in one sitting. It is important that you write speedily and with great abandon. Fling open the floodgates and spill out onto paper what is in your mind and soul. Be daring in your expression and pour out all that springs from the white heat of your conviction and enthusiasm. You probably will write two or three times as much as you will eventually use in your final speech. No doubt there will be many key phrases and expressions, whole paragraphs, and even sections that are overlooked in this first draft. The point is, you have something which is your product, marked by integrity, originality, and spontaneity. This becomes your working paper for much revising, condensation, rearranging, and deletion. Put this first creative outpouring of words aside for a few days until you can look at it with more detachment. Then pick it up and start working it over from beginning to end. You will now see, with a better sense of judgment, where you can use a more appropriate figure of speech, a fact or an example to support a point. You will find whole sections or paragraphs which may be omitted, or rewritten. You will find gaps which need to be filled in with examples or explanations. In this way you gradually upgrade the entire speech to attain brevity, coherence, unity, force, and cadence. Perhaps even your style will show through the lines. But don't be afraid to revise or rewrite the speech in its entirety. Remember, many great orators have been known to revise and rewrite their speeches as often as ten or fifteen times.

At this point you may also wish to choose a title for your oration. A formal title usually is necessary if you are to submit a complete, typewritten copy of the oration to the contest director or tournament officials. Furthermore, if the title of your oration is to be printed on the contest program or schedule of speeches, you will want a title which will stimulate the anticipation and interest of the audience and judges. A good title should meet at least three criteria. First, it should be relevant to the specific subject of your oration. It might even be a phrase or part of a quotation extracted from your oration. Second, it should be provocative and intriguing. It should arouse interest in the oration. A trite title may subconciously lead listeners to believe the oration itself will be dull. Third, it should be as brief as possible. Impact and "punch" are best gained by a short title.

5. *Memorize your speech.* You may ask, Why memorize since so few situations in life call for a memorized speech? Memorization helps you stay within the

time limit; it challenges you to know and master all the details; it helps preserve the literary quality of language; and it helps to reinforce and refine your delivery. Your situation is something like that of an actor. He must know his lines, yet knowing the lines is but a small part of being a great actor. Making meaning and emotions come alive is the heart of acting. The same is true for the orator who must lose himself so completely in thought and emotion that he doesn't have to think about the words. The finesse and polish of the whole performance is enhanced by memorization. Avoid a wooden, stilted, monotone delivery which reflects rote memorization of words devoid of living ideas.

In memorizing your speech you need not always be letter-perfect. Some find it helpful to start out by memorizing the ideas in their sequence. Once the thought line is firmly established in your mind, it is well to read the oration aloud twice from beginning to end with a five-minute interval of relaxation between the first and second readings. It will help the memorizing process to read with much vocal and bodily animation, with much emphasis on the thought and with exaggerated self-expression. This is a prelude to delivery. Start out by acting your part well, for it will help both memory and presentation. Usually the "whole" method is advisable when memorizing your oration. That is to say, you treat it orally as a single unit, from the first word to the final sentence. Always think the thought, not the words. Have a memorizing rehearsal two or three times a day, and at each rehearsal period go through the entire speech twice with a few minutes of relaxation between readings. It is also a good plan to go over the entire oration just before retiring at night and shortly after rising in the morning.

6. *Practice delivery.* Your final stages of memorization will probably overlap your delivery practice. The two processes should at this time be integrated. Delivery offers the final payoff for your efforts and should be the most enjoyable part of the entire experience. The role of delivery is much more important for the orator than for the debater, and in some contests it is one of the most important factors that determine victory or defeat. Delivery is discussed fully in Chapter 8.

CHAPTER 5

Thought and Content

ROLE OF THOUGHT IN HUMAN AFFAIRS

Consider for a moment the role of thought in the world in which we live. Thought is an indestructible force which moves the world and governs human action in the homes, shops, schools, churches, towns, court-rooms, legislative chambers—in fact, in every nook and corner of society. The power of an idea cannot be stopped by bullets, nor can it be confined by prison bars. Man has a mind that is turbulent, restless, and alert, and, like his heart, it never ceases to be active. The ability to think and produce ideas sets man apart from all other animals. It gives him a great capacity to adjust himself to his environment and enables him to build a better world for himself.

The lesson of history is clear. It teaches us that men who staked almost everything upon military or material force, as did Caesar, Alexander the Great, Napoleon, and Hitler, make a small impression upon the world compared to men who staked almost everything upon ideas, such as Plato, Newton, Milton, Galileo, Shake-speare, Einstein. We are familiar with the common practice of tyrants in government who, fearing the force of ideas, devise means to outlaw the free exchange of them. They outlaw freedom of speech and press, con-trive propaganda schemes, and build walls of one kind or another so that their brand of ideas may prevail within their borders. The battle lines of the cold war have been drawn to control the minds of people. No wonder the Russian Communists became expert at jamming the air channels of radio broadcasts from the free world! No wonder King Herod, who, upon hearing that the baby Jesus was being worshipped by his people, sent out the decree that all male babies in the land should be put to death! Of course, the great and mighty king, with all the armies at his command, was not afraid of one tiny baby. He was afraid the child would grow up with ideas opposed to his, so powerful as to topple him from his throne.

Thought is especially valuable and important to a free society. Freedom of speech and press is the life-blood of a democracy. Here lies the source of strength for our government and our nation. This fact provides an opportunity for the high school orator, and places a responsibility upon him, to energize and exchange worth-while ideas which will give our citizens added light and wisdom.

THE NATURE OF THOUGHT AND CONTENT

The words "thought" and "ideas" are often used interchangeably. Thought is the product of reasoning and the complex process of thinking, whereas an idea represents opinion, a point of view, an impression or notion about a thing, a person, an event or fact. When you say you have an "idea" of what a monkey is like, you say you have a mental image of a furry, four-limbed animal, very active and agile, with a long tail, making chattering noises, with face and eyes bearing some human semblance. Your image of the monkey is acquired through your senses. You have an image of something you want to do, such as getting a book from the library, attending a moving picture, or entering the oratorical contest. You may say you have a "notion" to do such and such. When you have a notion, you perceive a thing or a plan of action which is an indication that you have an idea.

You get your ideas from two major sources: the first is from your personal experience, your home, your friends, from people in general, your schooling or training, the things you have done, the attitudes and beliefs you have developed. There is also your day-dreaming and thought excursions which in total make up this first source of ideas lying within yourself.

The second source of ideas lies without yourself and is tapped by exploration and investigation. You look to what others know by reading, observation, conversation, and listening. You turn to newspapers, magazines, books, pamphlets, and listen to speeches and reports over radio and television. Vast storehouses of materials surround you. Libraries are especially useful, for in them rich substance prepared by able minds of various periods of time may be found.

The raw substance of your speech may be handled creatively in two general ways: by systematic mental effort or by vision or inspiration. Probably most of us use a combination of these two creative processes. Some ideas may be put together, piece by piece, like stones being fitted together to make a wall. This is often done in building a debate brief. Problem-solving thinking, which is often called "reflective thinking," usually follows a pattern of thought processes in this manner:

1. Find and locate a felt need or problem.

2. Become knowledgeable about the problem. Investigate, explore, and assemble pertinent data about it.

3. Examine and test possible suggested solutions.

4. Select one solution which seems best. Problem-solution orations are generally planned in this manner.

For most of us, the completed thought picture for an oration does not come to our minds like a "bolt out of the blue." Even when we do have a burst of inspiration or a sudden insight, we have already spent many agonizing hours stretching and straining the mind in an effort to break through a wall of bafflement and frustration. The inspiration of the moment is usually preceded by many long hours of perspiration.

THE ROLE OF THOUGHT AND CONTENT IN THE ORATION

An oration must represent more than beautiful phrases and a dramatic, polished delivery. Thought and content form the axis around which the oration revolves. Organization, language, and delivery must gravitate about it. When the content is excellent, it is easier to organize and write the oration. This also helps to build the speaker's confidence and motivate him in his delivery. The idea is the stuff out of which the oration must be fashioned. The big question in the judges' minds is, "Did the orator have something worth-while to say?" Of course, no one expects you to bring forth world-shaking ideas, but you are expected to show that you have made a sincere and genuine effort to master your subject. A careful and thorough search for truth is your first mission as an orator; your second mission is to reveal the truth by the spoken word in your most persuasive manner.

SOME GUIDES IN CHOOSING YOUR SUBJECT

Selecting a suitable subject is largely a matter of common sense. You will want to give the listeners something which will make them richer in spirit and better informed. Orations usually belong to the family of persuasive speeches. Three types of aims ordinarily characterize the persuasive speech:

1. In the first type, the aim is to impress or stimulate the listeners. The goal is to strengthen, reinforce, and renew a faith or belief which already exists in the minds of the audience. This type of speech grooves more deeply into the consciousness of the listener some salient truth or concept already accepted. The speech is faith-building and inspirational. While it may have elements of logical support, its aim is not so much to convince the mind as it is to reach the heart and soul of the listener, to bring him a rush of glad strength. Many sermons and memorial addresses are of this type. The Lincoln Gettysburg Address is an excellent example of the speech designed to impress.

2. In the second type of speech the aim is to convince, to make an idea believable and acceptable to the intellect. Such a speech is concerned with what is true

or false. It appeals to the objective, scientific mind, primarily by the use of sound evidence and logic. This is exactly what the tournament debater does when he seeks the favorable verdict of a single expert debate judge. In like manner, the lawyer, pleading his case before a single trained judge in court, seeks to convince the judge, primarily by use of facts and logic. His method would be quite different when speaking before a jury.

3. The aim of the third type of persuasive speech is to motivate the listener to act. This type of speech takes into account the deep wants and desires of the audience. Since most people are governed more by feelings than by reason, the weapons of persuasion are often used to exploit the masses for commercial or political gain. Psychologists and sociologists vary somewhat in their views as to what are the great underlying motives which determine human behavior. This subject is too complex to discuss here in detail; we can only touch on a few major considerations. Among the great dynamos which make people do things and which have a strong appeal are life, liberty, sex, religion, and curiosity. The Preamble to the Constitution places life and liberty at the top of the list. Life means food, clothing, shelter, and health. We have numerous laws dealing with housing, health, sanitation, gainful employment and living wages, and protection against crimes of violence. Freedom from want seems to be the everlasting cry. There is much talk about security from the cradle to the grave.

The idea of liberty springs from the human ego, from a sense of pride, from a feeling of self-respect, from the right and privilege to be somebody, even to be a "status-seeker." Patrick Henry brought it to a dramatic focus with the challenge, "Liberty or death!" Now the slogan is, "Better dead than red!" The phrase "Peace with honor" is a favorite among politicians, and it always makes good copy for newspaper headlines. Communism chooses bread over liberty and makes most of its gains where hunger pangs are the strongest.

The motive of sex represents a natural, deep, biological hunger. It manifests itself in love between man and woman and is the symbol of home and family, the cornerstone of our society.

Man, different from animals, has a spiritual side to his nature. No culture or nation ever existed without some form of religion. Many of the world's finest creative works in the arts—music, sculpture, painting, architecture, and literature—give us compelling testimony that religion is an answer to one of man's deepest needs.

Man, with his ability to think, has a desire to know. He is a curious creature. Curiosity, so evident in a child, never really dies, even with age. The hunger to learn and know can never be completely satisfied. Hence, the schoolhouse and the university will never vanish from a free society.

Motivation and emotional appeal in the oration usually do not stand out like a sore thumb. They are blended and integrated into the central idea with other means of manipulating the listener to action, such as attention devices, suggestion, speaker image, asthetic appeal in language, evidence, and reasoning.

The orator must always speak with a purpose. Speech communication is a two-way process, talking and listening. The orator must select his object as well as his subject. In fact, the object may often determine the subject. He must consider the dominant attitudes and beliefs of his listeners and adjust his speech in matter and manner with maximum audience satisfaction in mind. As he plans his approach, he should be guided by the question, "What in total will be most acceptable to judges and audience?" But also he must never compromise the *core* of his own basic position or beliefs.

We wish to point out that what is basically a matter of logic and what is basically emotional or motivational often cannot be sharply distinguished. What is logically sound may also be emotionally satisfying. Listeners tend to think and feel at the same time. What satisfies the intellect may also serve, in a large measure, to satisfy one's feelings. This is more likely to be true than to say, "What satisfies the feeling will also satisfy the intellect." Logic and emotion frequently cannot be separated, and one may not always detect how much of the impact from a certain point is due to logical substance and how much is based upon motivational substance.

Developing a Point or Basic Thought With a Definite Goal in Mind

A point is a unit of thought in your speech, one of the building blocks out of which it is constructed. The crux of your draftsmanship in building your oration lies in the way you develop and support your points and integrate them within the completed speech. Primarily, as a teaching or training aid, we suggest three questions related to three major purposes in the over-all treatment of specific sub-ideas or points: (1) Do you want the idea to be especially clear and easy to grasp? (2) Do you want to prove something is true; do you want the judicious listener to believe what you say? (3) Do you want to impress the listener or stir him to action?

These three goals are not always mutually exclusive, and one particular method of developing a specific point may fit under more than one goal. We will take up these three goals in three separate sections with brief discussions of them, supplemented by illustrative materials primarily from the orations in Part III to demonstrate various means of point development.

GOAL ONE—GET UNDERSTANDING
(Make it easy for the listener to grasp your meaning)

The goal of making an idea clear, although treated independently here, should also be a corollary goal in convincing and in persuading to action. However, at this time we wish to bring the problem of clarity into sharp focus. There are various ways in which you may develop a point to gain clarity. We list six for study and consideration:

1. Explain and define.
2. Tell a story.
3. Make comparisons and contrasts.
4. Translate the abstract into the concrete.
5. Divide and classify.
6. Be specific.

BUILDING THE CONTEST ORATION

1. *Explain and Define*

Speeches often fail to convey their intended meanings because the speaker fails to explain or define adequately certain key words he uses. Some words have multiple or complex meanings with a special meaning for the orator and a very different meaning for the audience. The customary ways of defining words are by the dictionary, by special authority, by derivation from the root of the word, by synonym, and by example.

2. *Tell a Story*

The story or illustration works on the principle of taking the listener from the unknown to the known. The story often has wide appeal and contains attention-getting elements such as suspense, surprise, and human interest. The kinds of illustrations are numerous, including fables, parables, figurative analogies, personal incidents, descriptions of people and events. The story should advance or clarify a point; it should be brief and in good taste and have the element of freshness or originality.

Patricia Ann Turner (Part III—"The Constitution—Temple of Liberty") uses a modern-day parable in her introduction to gain immediate audience interest and give insight into the basic theme of her oration.

Once there was a wise old hermit who lived in the hills of West Virginia. He was well known throughout the area for his philosophical insight and profound knowledge. One day some boys from a neighboring village decided to play a trick on the hermit to test his wisdom. They caught a bird and proceeded to the hermit's cave. One of the boys cupped the bird in his hands and called to the hermit, "Say old man, what is it I

62

have in my hands?" Hearing the chirping noise, the hermit said it was a bird. "Yes, but is it dead or alive?" asked the boy. If the hermit said the bird was alive, the boy would crush it in his hands. If the hermit said the bird was dead, the boy would open his hands and let the bird fly free. The hermit thought a moment and then replied, "It is what you make it."

3. *Make Comparisons and Contrasts*

Comparisons and contrasts may be in the form of an illustration and serve to set two ideas, incidents, or concepts side by side or one against the other. Such familiar phrases as "before and after," "the old and the new," and "now and then" suggest contrast. Moreover, this device frequently adds dramatic interest to a point.

Although his entire oration really involves contrasting the concepts of optimism and pessimism, Joseph Munoz (Part III—"Optimism") utilizes comparison and contrast for special clarity in one particular paragraph:

As today we recognize the necessity to isolate a deadly, infectious disease, so must we isolate attitudes and ideas like mine. Without optimism, what would this world be like? Pessimism can produce nothing but a spherical mass of dreary, ignorant, miserable people. But so long as there are optimistic people in this world, we are assured that there will always be smiles. So optimism is in part a "ray of light in a dark world." Optimism has a radiant contagion all its own wherever it is, in whatever situation it confronts. And, of a reverse nature is pessimism in its own limiting, debilitating way.

4. *Translate the Abstract into the Concrete*

The concrete is vivid and appeals to the senses. The abstract is vague and listeners are unable to pay attention for more than a minute or so to abstract thought, no matter how valuable or noble it may be. The word "death" is abstract, but "dead cat" is concrete. Likewise, "beauty" is abstract but a "red rose" is concrete.

The final two thirds of the oration by Janice Woelfle (Part III—"What Freedom Means to Me") involves making the abstract concepts of freedom and democracy as concrete as possible. One typical paragraph illustrates her method:

> Yes, democracy is voting in November, going to the church of our choice, speaking for what we feel is right, and being able to decide what we will read, see, hear, and do. But it is more than this. It is also the shout of a crowd as their team makes the final touchdown; it's the glow in the eyes of a little girl as she sits on Santa's knee; it's the joy on a three-year-old's face as he pretends that he's a boat in a mud puddle. It is the tender look on a mother's face as she gazes at her new-born child. She knows his future is insured because he was born in a free, democratic country.

5. *Divide and Classify*

To sort out objects or people into compartments or categories is a simple, age-old device. When a farmer says his barnyard is full of animals, it isn't very clear what he means, but if he says, "I have twenty-two pigs, nine cows, two horses, one hundred fifty chickens, two dogs and five cats," the pictures becomes much clearer.

In order to make the scope and nature of the business of agriculture more meaningful, John M. Mowrer (Part III—"A Great Future") divides and classifies agriculture into components:

> When totaled, nearly 40 per cent of existing jobs in America today are in agri-business, jobs vital to the well-being of

every American, jobs vital to our country. Agri-business encompasses more than five hundred occupations classified under seven major fields. These general fields include research, industry, education, communication, conservation, agri-service, and farming and ranching.

6. *Be Specific*

A good newspaper reporter must know how to get down to details, how to be definite and specific in telling the facts in his story. Crime detection is based largely on minute details, upon fingerprints, footprints, handwriting, and exactness of time and place, and so on. John M. Mowrer (Part III—"A Great Future") provides added insight into the business of agriculture by being specific rather than general:

This revolution brought drastic and meaningful changes to the face of America. The changes have continued until now, of the 65 million people employed in the United States, nearly 26 million are employed by agri-business, that industrial giant made up of the producers, processors, distributors, and service personnel for farm products. Nearly 8 million Americans work on farms and ranches, producing food and fiber; another 7 million are engaged in producing for and servicing these 8 million farmers. Eleven million workers process and distribute farm products, and close to one half million scientists are engaged in agri-business work.

GOAL TWO—CONVINCE THE MIND
(Get mental acceptance)

This goal for many would-be orators is often quite difficult, for it demands clear, logical thinking and an unemotional, calculating turn of mind. Your single purpose is to search for what is most likely to be the truth. What you say must be substantiated with reliable facts and cold, cogent logic. Imagine, if you can, that a line of argument in your oration must stand the test of trustworthiness and sound logic, not only at the present moment but five years hence. Theoretically, at least, try to put your feelings aside and appeal to a fair, impartial judge who is well informed on your subject.

Four standard and sound methods of supporting a point to establish the truth are the following:

1. Use specific instances and statistics.
2. Use literal analogies.
3. Use expert authority.
4. Use causal reasoning.

1. *Use Specific Instances and Statistics*

The role of specific instances and statistics in an oration is not as important as it is in a debate; however, examples can be used very effectively to nail down a key point. An oration should not be cluttered with a mass of evidence. It is usually best to select a few key instances which are chosen with care and placed at the points in your speech where they will be most effective. Above all, specific examples must be trustworthy and taken from reliable and competent sources. They should be pertinent to the contention you wish to prove. Statistics (which organize and evaluate a mass of specific instances) should cover sufficient cases and length of time, be based on units typical of the whole group, come from reliable sources, be relevant, and be made meaningful to the audience.

To establish the type of persecution with which his oration deals, Joel Swabb (Part III—"The Irresponsibles") cites a specific instance concerning his high school Problems of Democracy teacher:

> The time is 11 A.M. A school teacher in Pittsburgh, Pennsylvania, sits behind her desk opening the morning mail. She has just received a letter from a friend in New York, a copy of *Time* magazine, and a plain white mailing envelope with no return address. A quick slip of the letter opener and she is greeted with the bright red exclamation, "Communist."

Mr. Swabb employs a number of other specific examples in his oration to reinforce or prove particular points. Throughout his oration, John M. Mowrer (Part III—"A Great Future") makes extensive yet meaningful use of various kinds of statistical evidence to prove his points. This entire oration should be read in order to gain insight into the effective use of statistics. In addition, Stephen Alan Oxman (Part III—"A List") uses statistics in the form of percentages in a public opinion poll.

2. *Use Literal Analogies*

The literal analogy is used to draw comparisons between two items, people, situations, and so forth, which are alike in their essentials in order to prove an unknown facet of one of them. There must be no important differences between the things compared.

In a debate at the Virginia Ratifying Convention on whether to ratify the proposed American Constitution, Patrick Henry (June 5, 1788) used a literal analogy to prove that the American states could successfully exist as a loose confederation. He argued against the strong central government provided for in the proposed Constitution:

> The history of Switzerland clearly proves that we might be in amicable alliance with those states without adopting this Constitution. Switzerland is a confederacy, consisting of dissimilar governments. This is an example which proves that governments of dissimilar structures may be confederated. That confederate republic has stood upwards of four hundred years; and, although several of the individual republics are democratic, and the rest aristocratic, no evil has resulted from this dissimilarity; for they have braved all the power of France and Germany during that long period.

On the following day, however, James Madison questioned the analogy on the basis of significant differences between the nations. He said:

> With respect to the Swiss, whom the honorable gentleman has proposed for our example, as far as historical authority may be relied on, we shall find their government quite unworthy of our imitation. I am sure, if the honorable gentleman had adverted to their history and government, he never would have quoted their example here; he would have found that, instead of respecting the rights of mankind, their government (at least several of their cantons) is one of the vilest aristocracies that ever was instituted: the peasants of some of their cantons are more oppressed and degraded than the subjects of any monarch in Europe. . . . As we are not circumstanced like them, no conclusive precedent can be drawn from their situation.

Who do you think was more correct, Henry or Madison?

3. *Use Expert Authority*

The absolute authority, the one that is 100 per cent perfect, is rare indeed. We must, therefore, search and use the best possible authority we can find. The most desirable authority should meet the following requirements: (1) He should not be biased for or against the thing being considered; (2) he should be a qualified expert in the field about which he is quoted; (3) he should be demonstrably well informed on the subject on which he is quoted; (4) his testimony should be acceptable to the audience. It usually is wise to tell the audience something about the qualifications of the expert you quote.

To bolster his basic point that lack of true communication and understanding is at the root of many of mankind's ills, Carl W. Carmichael (Part III—"One Man in His Time") cites the expert testimony of Benjamin E. Mays, Negro president of Morehouse College in Atlanta, Georgia: "The plain truth is that Negroes and white people in the South never had honest communication. Honest communication is built on truth and integrity; and upon respect of the one for the other." But one might consider whether Dr. Mays fully meets all four tests of expert authority discussed above; or does he qualify in some respects but not in others?

4. Use Causal Reasoning

It is often claimed that nothing in this world exists by pure chance, that there is a cause for everything. The orator will find causal reasoning most useful. There are two main types of causal reasoning: (1) effect to cause and (2) cause to effect. One looks to what probably has happened, the other to what probably will happen. "Why" is the big word when we seek the cause or effect. Why the fire? Why the train wreck? Why was the bus late? What was the shooting for? and so on. Every child knows something about this type of reasoning. He has heard this question time and time again from his parents, "Johnny, why are you home so late?" "Why don't you eat?" "Why did you?" and "Why don't you?" A single simple reason can seldom be given. There are usually many causes, and we try to put our finger on the primary cause. If we search for the most probable cause, we should ask two questions: (1) Is the cause named adequate to produce the effect? (2) Could other causes intervene and produce the same effect?

In the forward look, when we consider cause to effect, we in a sense turn prophet. We look to the probable outcome and make an educated guess. In this form of reasoning, we should ask: (1) Is the cause sufficient to produce the named effect? (2) Is the cause prevented from producing the named effect?

Both types of casual reasoning, effect-to-cause and cause-to-effect, are employed by Stephen Alan Oxman (Part III—"A List"). First of all he examines the various wars of past history (effects) in order to determine their generating principle or cause:

> For if you look at all the wars of all the ages, if you look at all the strife between men, you discover a universal cause— one man or group of men has infringed upon the *basic rights* of another man or group of men. It all boils down to that—one man infringing upon the *basic rights* of another. The inevitable result has been war.

Then he reasons from restrictions on American freedoms and rights (cause) to their probable end results (effects):

All men are created equal. Oh! But this is the Cold War. Everything endangers the national security! Maybe it should be, "All men are created equal *except* Communists and Nazis." But where do we stop? What is to prevent it from becoming "All men are created equal *except* Communists and Nazis and Catholics and Jews and Democrats and Republicans—STOP! When you start qualifying freedom these ways, when you start qualifying freedom as did the high school students in that opinion poll, when you start *qualifying freedom*—WATCH OUT! for what happens to *you*.

GOAL THREE—IMPRESS OR MOTIVATE TO ACTION

The goals to impress and motivate to action, in many respects, have much in common. Rather than make two separate categories under Goal Three, we will combine the purposes of impressing and activating. In the speech intended to impress, the orator aims to make his ideas stick in the mind of the listener. In other words, his aim is to make his message unforgettable. This is particularly challenging to his creative imagination. In the speech designed to move the will of the listener to action, special devices to impress are frequently used and integrated with devices designed to get action. The persuasive speech employing motivational and other tactics to influence behavior is among the most complex of all forms of speech-making. This type of speech tends to be in total more psychological than logical. Following are some of the standard methods used to impress the listener and to motivate him to act:

71

BUILDING THE CONTEST ORATION

1. *Striking Comparisons and Contrasts*

One of the best ways to make your ideas stick in the mind of the listener is to use a striking comparison or contrast. If you cite a lot of facts and figures without relating them to anything, the listener won't be very interested. If you say there are over one million freight cars on our railroads, the fact may not make much of an impression upon your audience. But suppose you say, "Connect all the freight cars into one long train; imagine that train roaring through your town at the rate of sixty miles per hour. It would take three weeks before you would see the lights of the caboose." This would have greater impact.

In order to impress upon the audience more clearly the true economic importance of agriculture, John M. Mowrer (Part III—"A Great Future") compares the financial assets of farmers to those of all American corporations:

> The last of these categories, farming and ranching, alone is definitely big business, for the farm today requires an average investment of over $43,000. The total assets of farmers is an astounding $200 billion, a figure equal to three fourths the total assets of all the corporations in the United States.

2. *The Dramatic Story*

The dramatic story is a sure-fire device to heighten the interest and attention of the audience and at the same time arouse feelings to make a point more impressive. In his famous oration "The New South," Henry W. Grady (December 22, 1886) painted this stirring picture of the weary, defeated, yet proud Southern soldier returning home after the Civil War:

Will you bear with me while I tell you of another army that sought its home at the close of the late war—an army that marched home in defeat and not in victory—in pathos and not in splendor, but in glory that equaled yours, and to hearts as loving as ever welcomed heroes home. Let me picture to you the footsore Confederate soldier, as, buttoning up in his faded gray jacket the parole which was to bear testimony to his children of his fidelity and faith, he turned his face southward from Appomattox in April, 1865. Think of him as ragged, half-starved, heavy-hearted, enfeebled by want and wounds; having fought to exhaustion, he surrenders his gun, wrings the hands of his comrades in silence, and, lifting his tear-stained and pallid face for the last time to the graves that dot the old Virginia hills, pulls his gray cap over his brow and begins the slow and painful journey.

In the entire first third of her oration, Janice Woelfle (Part III—"What Freedom Means to Me") relates a dramatic narrative based on a meeting between three Americans and a cautious Soviet citizen in Russia. She uses this dramatic story to drive home at the outset her basic point concerning the universal value attached to freedom. And Joel Swabb (Part III—"The Irresponsibles") uses a dramatic story to depict vividly the "confidence" which Americans should have in their democratic way of life:

I have seen the results of the "confidence" which President Kennedy so strongly urges us to demonstrate. A few weeks ago a top-ranking member of the American Communist Party came to our campus to debate Dr. Charles Layton on the merits of communism. Before he arrived, the far right began to act. Some threatened to cancel their financial pledges to the

73

college; others indicted the administration for providing a foothold for an agent of a foreign power. But the college leaders held firm. What was the result of this encounter between one of communism's ablest spokesmen and a distinguished professor of speech? How foolish and unappealing communism looked to the one thousand people who had assembled on that January night. When it was over the soundly defeated Communist debater turned to his opponent and said: "You were a gentleman, but you hit awfully hard."

3. *The Personalized Story*

Occasionally the personalized story can be very fitting and appropriate for the orator. Personal words are direct, sincere, and realistic. Abraham Lincoln's farewell address at Springfield is an excellent example of the personalized story.

The results of lack of effective communication are pictured by Carl W. Carmichael (Part III—"One Man in His Time"). The personal experience he relates in the introduction of his oration clearly points to his central message:

. . . I met a man three summers ago at the mental hospital where I worked. As he limply climbed onto the soda fountain stool I could see he had been beaten. His right eye was blackened and almost closed. His left arm in a sling seemed to point to the purple welts on his neck and face. He said, "Nobody understands me," then ordered an ice cream soda. I gave him the soda but I couldn't tell him that he was right. Whoever had beaten him didn't understand him. Men fear what they don't understand.

4. *Use of the Rhetorical Question*

The rhetorical question is an invitation and a challenge to the listener to think and supply an answer.

You are not expected to spell out the answer immediately and specifically. Your question helps to dramatize a point and prod the listener to think and feel on his own. Note how Patrick Henry (March 23, 1775) used the rhetorical question to advantage:

> They tell us, sir, that we are weak; unable to cope with so formidable an adversary. But when shall we be stronger? Will it be the next week, or the next year? Will it be when we are totally disarmed, and when a British guard shall be stationed in every house? Shall we gather strength by irresolution and inaction? Shall we acquire the means of effectual resistance by lying supinely on our backs, and hugging the delusive phantom of hope, until our enemies shall have bound us hand and foot? Sir, we are not weak, if we make proper use of the means which the God of nature hath placed in our power.

Carl W. Carmichael (Part III—"One Man in His Time") makes compelling use of rhetorical questions to stimulate the audience's thought pattern toward the central thesis of his oration: "But what is communication? A man speaking? A transference of ideas? Or a complete understanding of attitudes—sincerity, honesty, truth?" John M. Mowrer (Part III—"A Great Future") uses three simple rhetorical questions to enumerate the central topics of his oration on American agriculture: "What is it? What has happened to it? And what does the future really hold?"

5. *Quoting Popular Authorities*

We are all familiar with the way national advertisers use popular people to endorse and recommend all kinds of products. This is a simple device enabling one to appear to be on the side of heroes and celebrated personages. The orator, however, must be more careful and use more discretion than the advertisers of soaps, pills, and hair tonic. He must show more sincerity and integrity than we see in a television commercial. There must be reverence and respect for the source he quotes which usually is from a work of literature, the Bible, the Constitution, a great patriot, a well known educator, or the like.

Patricia Ann Turner (Part III—"The Constitution —Temple of Liberty") relies heavily on citations of opinions from popular authorities. In her oration, the ideas and opinions of the following famous people are cited: George Washington, Benjamin Franklin, Thomas Jefferson, William Ewart Gladstone, and John F. Kennedy. Their opinions are used to impress and motivate the listener; Miss Turner's purpose is to inspire.

6. *Repetition and Refrain*

You do not drive a nail into a board with one single stroke but by repeated blows of the hammer. Key phrases in television commercials are repeated, perhaps six times in sixty seconds. Repetition and restatement aid audience comprehension and retention of basic ideas. The orator, when using this device, must use restraint and not overdo it; too much repetition leads to triteness and boredom. Note the skill with which Prime Minister Winston Churchill (June 4, 1940) used this technique during England's darkest hour following the defeat at Dunkirk:

The British Empire and the French Republic, linked together in their cause and in their need, will defend to the death their native soil, aiding each other like good comrades to the utmost of their strength. Even though large tracts of Europe and many old and famous States have fallen or may fall into the grip of the Gestapo and all the odious apparatus of Nazi rule, we shall not flag or fail. We shall go on to the end, we shall fight in France, we shall fight on the seas and oceans, we shall fight with growing confidence and growing strength in the air, we shall defend our Island, whatever the cost may be, we shall fight on the beaches, we shall fight on the landing grounds, we shall fight in the fields and in the streets, we shall fight in the hills; we shall never surrender.

Stephen Alan Oxman (Part III—"A List") uses repetition and refrain based on the title of his oration. His use of repetition in the introductory paragraphs gives meaning and impact to the title of his speech:

But to say that man has the right to life, liberty and the pursuit of happiness is to say a million things. It means he has the freedom to speak, the freedom to think, the freedom to go where he wants, the freedom to laugh, the freedom to be left alone, and so many other freedoms that it would be impossible to *list* them all.

There was, however, in the latter part of the eighteenth century in America, a group of men who did *list* some of the basic rights embodied in the Grand Right to life, liberty, and the pursuit of happiness. The *list* that these men made is perhaps the most important *list* in history.

7. *Appeal to Basic Human Nature*

The orator can appeal to a deep human desire or a sense of moral values. Man does not live by bread alone. He has a spiritual, idealistic, humanitarian side to his nature. The orator must be sensitive to the listener's soul as well as to his purely materialistic interests.

An appeal to one facet of human nature is made by Stephen Alan Oxman (Part III—"A List") when he combines repetition with an appeal to man's sense of individual responsibility:

> It is a question of *individual responsibility*. One individual assuming the responsibility to respect, protect and cherish not only his *basic rights* but those of his fellow man. Only when this doctrine of *individual responsibility* has been spread far enough and wide enough until it is at the top of men's hearts and minds everywhere, will man have the *freedom not to worry about his freedom*. Only then will it be unnecessary to make a LIST as did our forefathers, for fear that someone would take away their basic rights. And only then, when this doctrine of *individual responsibility* has been spread far enough and wide enough until it is at the top of men's hearts and minds everywhere, will man have solved the greatest problem he has ever known—*learning how to live together*, yes, together, in kindness, in justice, in mutual respect, in peace, in love—Russian with American, black with white, man with man.

In a less obvious way, Carl W. Carmichael (Part III —"One Man in His Time") concludes his oration with an appeal to duty and individual responsibility:

> One man in his time plays many parts. You are that man. This is the time. Whatever part you play, are you communicating understanding through your attitudes? Whether in the world, or in the nation, or in your own home town— understanding must be brought about by communication on the level that all people can understand. The success of communication today is dependent on your attitudes.

8. *Imagery*

Imagery is a means of awakening and stimulating the imagination. It generates ideas through vivid mental pictures and helps to awaken deeper feelings. It often serves as an effective method for impressing a vivid picture upon the listener's mind. Examples of effective use of imagery are legion among American orators. For further comments on imagery, see Chapter 7.

Patricia Ann Turner (Part III—"The Constitution —Temple of Liberty") employs imagery at several points. At the signing of the American Constitution, she relates, "Thirty-nine gentlemen in silk stockings, knee breeches, and ruffled shirts signed the document." She depicts the Statue of Liberty in New York Harbor:

> The right hand holds a great torch high in the air, while the left hand grasps a tablet bearing the date of the Declaration of Independence. A broken chain at her feet symbolizes the bonds which chain a people struggling for their freedom. At night the torch in the right hand gleams with light . . . a symbol of liberty shedding light upon the world.

CHAPTER 6

Giving the Oration Shape and Form

The idea of an orderly universe emerges clearly in the story of Creation as told in the Bible. Its opening words are: "In the beginning God created the heaven and the earth. And the earth was without form, and void." Out of chaos emerge form and order for a physical world and its vast kingdom of plants and animals. Thus, form and order is the first law of nature. Every insect, every tree, every blade of grass has its intricate and delicate pattern of form and structure.

Form is the artist's law. A painting must be based on an orderly plan, a design, and must give its central impression. The same law applies to architecture, sculpture, music, poetry, oratory, and so on. The creative act of man, whether it be a house, a poem, a mousetrap, or an oration, embraces in various ways this dimension of form and order. In his *Phaedrus*, Plato urges that "every discourse, like a living creature, should be so put together that it has its own body and lacks neither head nor feet, middle nor extremities, all composed in such a way that they suit both each other and the whole."

Form is especially important to the orator, *for it is a means to an end*. It helps to make ideas clear, attractive, and effective. Many speakers with worth-while ideas and effective delivery still fail because of their rambling, disconnected discourse which only confuses their listeners.

Let us explain more fully what we mean by the use of a story about an elderly, mild-mannered judge who became famous for winning prizes at flower shows. One day a friend complimented the judge on his beautiful rose exhibits and congratulated him upon his success. The friend was amazed at his reply: "Why, my roses aren't more beautiful than the others. The roses themselves don't win prizes; it is the way they look to the judges, and my wife takes care of that. There are a lot of roses better than mine, but they are stuck haphazardly into old fruit jars and milk cans. Some of them are squeezed together so that you hate to look at them. But my wife knows just how to arrange roses so they look even more beautiful than they are."

Later, the judge told his friend how the roses taught him a lesson about courtroom speeches. He pointed out how many lawyers, with fine arguments and plenty of evidence, often failed because they did not know how to select and arrange their materials. And he told how, on the other hand, he had seen lawyers win cases with meager facts because they were experts at arranging and organizing them. We might go on and point out how many contest orators fall short of the mark because they take beautiful ideas and jam them, so to speak, into milk bottles, and how thousands of speakers fail before their clubs and committees because they carelessly jam their ideas into ugly glass fruit jars.

You must organize the oration for the same reason you plan for any undertaking, whether it be building a house or a bridge, or playing a game of checkers. We organize to get a particular job done more effectively. When it comes to building the oration, organization means order instead of chaos, clarity instead of haziness, force instead of weakness, beauty instead of ugliness, efficiency instead of waste.

Unfortunately, we cannot offer a simple, fixed, detailed, all-purpose formula for organizing your oration. The plan and design of your speech is an individual undertaking. Each oration is a separate, individual case with its own unique problems of organization, which are governed by the kind of subject you have, your supporting materials, your ability in logical analysis, your creative imagination, your audience, the occasion, and your sensitivity to aesthetic, emotional, and logical values. The oration must stand as a creative piece, designed and tailored fresh and new to suit the speaker, the subject, and its purpose.

There are underlying laws which usually help your oration to stand as a creative product. We refer to the laws of unity, coherence, balance and proportion, clarity and force.

It is best to have one dominant, central idea, one dominant mood and one purpose. A Christmas tree that looks like two trees violates the law of unity.

It is best that sub-ideas hang together like grapes on the vine. Essential facts, examples, and images should be related to the central theme and purpose.

It is best that the ideas which go to make up the central message be so arranged and emphasized as to give balance and proportion to the total effect. The lopsided Christmas tree, with thick, heavy branches and needles in one place and none in another, looks ugly and out of proportion.

It is best that the organization of the oration serve to make the main theme clear and easy to understand. The structure of the speech should give the listener a clear thought picture.

It is best that ideas be arranged to increase the intensity of the listener's interest and his motivational response. The structure of the speech, with its sequence of ideas, should build toward a forceful climax. The structure should be cumulative in its communication impact upon the listener.

PATTERNS OF GENERAL STRUCTURE

The old pattern of organization most familiar to us, learned in English composition lessons, is that of the introduction, body, and conclusion. This has sometimes been even more simplified by the backwoods preacher who says a speech must have a beginning, middle, and end. Of course, these three parts usually are not as distinctly discernible as the three parts of a house, namely, foundation, floors, and roof, or the three parts of a cow —head, body, and tail.

For the sake of clarity and simplicity, we will consider for the moment some traditional concepts about the role of the introduction, body, and conclusion.

Introduction

Among the major functions of the introduction are the following:

1. To enlist the attention and interest of the audience.

2. To prepare the audience for a clear understanding of what you are going to say.

3. To lead the audience to appreciate the importance and value of your subject, and whet the appetite for what is coming.

4. To win the good will of the audience for yourself and your subject; to develop a favorable state of mind in your listeners. You may have to overcome hostility or prejudices against your subject.

In simple terms, the central purpose of the introduction is to pave the way for what you have to say. Get the listener in tune mentally and emotionally for the message. We do not mean to say every introduction should perform all the above functions, but two or more of them usually are pertinent in any introduction.

Body

The body is the heart of the speech. Here you unfold and develop your thesis or main line of thought. Here you lay out and fully display the product of your mind as it is related to your subject.

Conclusion

The functions of the conclusion will, of course, vary from oration to oration. Here are some of the more common functions:

1. To end the speech. There must be a finish, a

signing off. The audience should sense that the oration has been completed.

2. To re-emphasize and drive home the central idea.

3. To summarize and reclarify the highlights of the central idea.

4. To dramatize and ennoble the main idea and its purpose. Lift the listener out of his seat.

A combination of two or more of these functions is usually present in any oration. The type of conclusion which is dominant will vary from one oration to another.

A Few Warning Signals

We have briefly mentioned some basic guidelines or principles for the introduction and conclusion. We will now point out some common errors or faults observed among contest orators.

Beware of these dangers in your introduction:

1. The introduction should not be too long or drawn out.

2. The means used to gain attention should be in good taste, should not be too dramatic or sensational.

3. The introduction should not be misleading; it should not suggest a central thought-line other than the one you will offer.

Beware of these dangers in your conclusion:

1. Avoid the anticlimax. Once you have hit the high point, don't try to regain it during the closing

moments unless you are sure you can surpass it. You may spoil the initial communication impact you have gained.

2. Avoid the drawn-out ending. The ending should be definite and sharp. A few added or tacked-on sentences will spoil the effect of a clean-cut finish.

3. Avoid too much repetition of the obvious. This makes you guilty of redundancy.

A Five-Step Formula for Organizing the Oration

We present a suggested organization pattern with five steps in logical, motivated sequence, a pattern which generally is usable in building your oration and in other speeches designed to convince, impress, or activate the listener. These steps, in most instances, can be identified in sales talks, promotional talks, political speeches, and in persuasive speeches in general. Under each step we list an inventory of methods which might be used. This is a reservoir of devices; therefore, only some of them may be applicable for a particular oration. We present these steps in a condensed outline form, followed by some examples to show how the pattern has been applied in some well-known speeches and, in a measure, to show how the pattern fits some orations in Part III.

1. *Make contact with the listener (get his attention).*

    Methods: a. Start off with a dramatic, startling statement or example.

                  b. Use a quotation from a famous book or man.

   c. Use a slogan or phrase as a key to your central idea or purpose.
   d. Refer to a top news event or historical incident.
   e. Relate a personal incident.
   f. Ask a leading question from which the main idea may unfold.
   g. Tastefully compliment the audience.
   h. Give tribute to a worthy cause on which you and your audience are in full accord.
   i. Emphasize goals, ideals, values, experiences, etc., common to both yourself and the particular audience.

2. *Tell why the subject is important (justification).*

   Methods: a. Tell why the subject is of special interest and concern to you.
   b. Tell why the subject should interest and concern the audience.
   c. Tell why you have earned the right to talk on this subject.
   d. Use a striking fact or event to throw the public spotlight on your topic.
   e. Indicate or allude to your central purpose.

3. *Reveal the thesis or central idea (get to your text).*

   Methods: a. Make an outright declaration of what your speech is about.

      b. Explain, define, clarify the meaning of your central idea.

      c. Use a question or questions embracing answers which develop the main line of thought.

      d. Indicate the large compartments of your speech. Name the pegs upon which you will hang the key points.

      e. If you use the screened attack, be sure to keep your central purpose well guarded.

4. *Establish belief or attitude. Develop and unfold your central thought picture (visualize the need).*

    Methods: a. Explain and define.

               b. Use statistical evidence.

               c. Cite examples and illustrations.

               d. Use analogies.

               e. Quote authorities.

               f. Tell a story laden with evidence.

               g. Show causal relation in reasoning.

               h. Dramatize an idea.

5. *Show what to do, arrive at conclusions, interpret values (application step).*

    Methods: a. Show how a difficulty may be resolved.

               b. Propose a definite course of action.

               c. Generate new light, present a new interpretation.

d. Drive home the central idea.
e. Summarize to make the meaning clear.
f. Idealize and ennoble the central idea.
g. Make a categorical, 1-2-3 type of summary.
h. Leave audience with a satisfied feeling.
i. Close the speech; create the sense of its completion.

EXAMPLES OF HOW THE FORMULAS HAVE BEEN USED

The Gettysburg Address by Abraham Lincoln

1. Contact Step

Fourscore and seven years ago our fathers brought forth on this continent a new nation, conceived in liberty, and dedicated to the proposition that all men are created equal.

2. Justification Step

Now we are engaged in a great civil war, testing whether that nation, or any nation so conceived and so dedicated, can long endure. We are met on a great battlefield of that war.

3. Introduce Subject Step

We have come to dedicate a portion of that field as a final resting place for those who here gave their lives that that nation might live. It is altogether fitting and proper that we should do this.

4. Establish Belief Step

But, in a larger sense, we cannot dedicate—we cannot consecrate—we cannot hallow—this ground. The brave men, living and dead, who struggled here, have consecrated it, far above our poor power to add or detract. The world will little note, nor long remember, what we say here, but it can never forget what they did here.

5. *Application Step*

It is for us the living, rather, to be dedicated here to the unfinished work which they who fought here have thus far so nobly advanced. It is rather for us to be here dedicated to the great task remaining before us—that from these honored dead we take increased devotion to that cause for which they gave the last full measure of devotion—that we here highly resolve that these dead shall not have died in vain—that this nation, under God, shall have a new birth of freedom and that government of the people, by the people, for the people, shall not perish from the earth.

Declaration of War by Franklin D. Roosevelt

1. *Contact Step*

(Reference to Pearl Harbor attack)

Yesterday, December 7, 1941—a date which will live in infamy—the United States of America was suddenly and deliberately attacked by naval and air forces of the empire of Japan.

2. *Justification Step*

(Our State Department made every effort to keep the peace)

The United States was at peace with that nation and, at the solicitation of Japan, was still in conversation with its Government and its Emperor looking toward the maintenance of peace in the Pacific.

Indeed, one hour after Japanese air squadrons had commenced bombing Oahu, the Japanese Ambassador to the United States and his colleague delivered to the Secretary of State a formal reply to a recent American message. While this reply stated that it seemed useless to continue the existing diplomatic negotiations, it contained no threat or hint of war or armed attack.

3. *Introduce Subject Step*

   (This attack was deliberately planned)

It will be recorded that the distance of Hawaii from Japan makes it obvious that the attack was deliberately planned many days or even weeks ago. During the intervening time, the Japanese Government has deliberately sought to deceive the United States by false statements and expressions of hope for continued peace.

4. *Establish Belief Step*

   (Damage was great. Other attacks also launched. Hostilities exist. Our lives and safety in danger. We will remember it.)

The attack yesterday on the Hawaiian Islands has caused severe damage to American naval and military forces. Very many American lives have been lost. In addition, American ships have been reported torpedoed on the high seas between San Francisco and Honolulu.

Yesterday the Japanese Government also launched an attack against Malaya.

Last night Japanese forces attacked Hong Kong.

Last night Japanese forces attacked Guam.

Last night Japanese forces attacked the Philippine Islands.

Last night the Japanese attacked Wake Island.

This morning the Japanese attacked Midway Island.

Japan has, therefore, undertaken a surprise offensive extending throughout the Pacific area. The facts of yesterday speak for themselves. The people of the United States have already formed their opinions and well understand the implications to the very life and safety of our nation.

As Commander in Chief of the Army and Navy I have directed that all measures be taken for our defense.

Always will we remember the character of the onslaught against us.

5. *Application Step*

(We will win. I ask Congress to declare war.)

No matter how long it may take us to overcome this premeditated invasion, the American people in their righteous might will win through to absolute victory.

I believe I interpret the will of the Congress and of the people when I assert that we will not only defend ourselves to the uttermost but will make very certain that this form of treachery shall never endanger us again.

Hostilities exist. There is no blinking at the fact that our people, our territory and our interests are in grave danger.

With confidence in our armed forces—with the unbounding determination of our people—we will gain the inevitable triumph—so help us God.

I ask that the Congress declare that since the unprovoked and dastardly attack by Japan on Sunday, December 7, a state of war has existed between the United States and the Japanese Empire.

Although all of the winning contest orations in Part III of this book contain introductions, bodies, and conclusions, and although some of them reflect the general problem-solution mode of arrangement, two of the orations particularly illustrate the five-step sequence of contact, justification, thesis, belief, and application.

The first three paragraphs of Joel Swabb's oration, "The Irresponsibles," establish contact with the audience. Through the use of three dramatic examples, he seizes the audience's attention, whets their appetite for what is coming, and leads towards his central idea. In the fourth paragraph, he justifies the importance of his topic, rightist extremist groups, by citing testimony which relates it to the audience and by explaining his own personal involvement with the topic. Paragraphs five and six present his thesis or central idea: That rightist extremism leads to oversimplification of problems and solutions, to a detachment from reality and rationality, and to undemocratic behavior. He elaborates his thesis through declarative statements and through a rhetorical question which channels thought. In paragraphs seven through ten, Swabb establishes the belief, the need, he desires to depict. Through specific examples, extended illustration, and citation of testimony he establishes that something must be done about rightist extremism. Then in the final paragraphs, eleven through thirteen, he presents the application step. Wisely he recognizes that the solution to the problem is not simple. He merely offers one suggestion, one course of action, which would be useful: Confidence, faith in the American ideals which promote trust in the dignity of man. Swabb gives an example of this confidence at work and then moves to his final paragraph ending on a note of finality, and re-emphasizing the idea that Americans must stand *for* rather than *against* something.

BUILDING THE CONTEST ORATION

The contact and justification steps are combined in the first two paragraphs of Carl W. Carmichael's oration, "One Man in His Time." Through imagery and personal example he secures attention. He justifies his topic, lack of communication, and leads toward his central idea. The third paragraph contains, in question form, his thesis: Lack of communication is rooted in lack of sincere and honest understanding of attitudes. Paragraphs four through nine aim at establishing belief in the need for effective communication, for fuller understanding. To establish this belief, he utilizes examples, cites testimony, dramatizes ideas, adapts a quotation from Shakespeare, and cites a pertinent bit of poetry by Thomas Hardy. He presents the application step in paragraphs ten through twelve. Examples again are employed. Paragraph eleven contains his specific three-point solution for combating the problem. And in the final paragraph he places responsibility squarely on the audience's shoulders. Also he summarizes and drives home his central idea: "The success of communication today is dependent on your attitudes."

PATTERNS OF ARRANGEMENT

Having discussed some patterns of the structure of your oration, we will now discuss the arrangement of ideas and materials within the oration itself. Obviously, the arrangement of your ideas will be governed partly by your central purpose, partly by your specific purpose at a given place in your speech, partly by the kind of supporting materials used, and partly by the form of discourse used, such as narration, description, exposition, and argumentation.

Some of the more common and traditional patterns for arranging ideas and thought materials are as follows:

1. The natural order
2. The compartment or catalogue order
3. The "why" order
4. The "common relationship" order
5. The problem-solution order
6. The compelling order

1. *The Natural Order (time, place, motion)*

Nature plays a hand in everything in the world about us. There are the ever-present and dominant factors of time, place, and motion. The day, the month, the year, and the seasons fall into familiar divisions of time. The country road, hills, valleys, forest, rivers, lakes, houses, and so forth are the ever-present outlines of space and place. These things may be discussed according to various standard patterns: north, south, east, west; left to right; inside to outside; past to present to future, etc. The city traffic, speeding trains, the ocean waves, people walking, dogs running, birds flying, and so forth, remind us that we live in a world of motion. The story begins, "once upon a time." Lincoln's Gettysburg Address moves from the past to the present to the future.

As we consider this pattern of development, there are two points to keep in mind: first, there is a natural, logical sequence of ideas. There is really little to figure out. Everything falls into line naturally. Try not to upset the law of nature. If you are making a speech about the life of Thomas Jefferson, you begin with his birth and early childhood and end with the old age and death of the great spokesman of liberty. The second point is to remember that these factors of time, place, and motion commonly do not prevail throughout the entire oration, but form a segment or part of your speech.

2. *The Compartment or Catalogue Order*

This pattern concerns the classification of ideas and materials. It puts things into categories and helps to make the thought easy to understand. It is a device for sorting materials and ideas into separate piles and naming them one by one. Suppose a speaker is developing a central thesis about our national security in time of war. It would be helpful to show that we, as a nation, must be strong on four fronts: the military, the political, the economic, and the psychological. Speakers often refer to our government as being divided into three branches—legislative, executive, and judicial. This pattern of thought arrangement is one of the most common of all for the orator.

Carl W. Carmichael (Part III—"One Man in His Time") adapts the categories implied in a quotation from Shakespeare in order to structure the major part of the body or "belief step" of his oration. The many parts which one man in his time plays are thus used as topic ideas in four consecutive paragraphs. The schoolboy, the soldier, the politician, and the businessman are the categories discussed by Carmichael.

3. The "Why" Order (cause and effect)

Philosophers tell us that nothing exists without cause. We are constantly asking why things happen, why people do things, why we should have a law or an ordinance for this or that. There is sudden death, followed by an autopsy to find the cause of death. You have a stomach ache and you ask what brought this on. Causal thought has already been discussed and illustrated in the preceding chapter.

4. The "Common Relationship" Order (points similar in kind)

Often, for the sake of clarity or emphasis, points may be effectively grouped under one common heading. This helps to make ideas more impressive and unforgettable. It is common in sermons, inspirational and persuasive talks. This is exemplified by the three S's of the Salvation Army—Soup, Soap and Salvation; by the three R's of education—Reading, wRiting, and aRithmetic; and the four H's of the Club—Head, Heart, Health, and Hands. The Four Freedoms speech by Franklin D. Roosevelt exemplified this relationship order. This pattern also demonstrates the compartment or catalog order, but it is applied in a special manner.

5. The Problem-Solution Order

This is a natural, logical pattern commonly used in orations and all kinds of persuasive speeches. The law of logic dictates this pattern. A problem is located, identified, and urgency of need established. Out of this need picture grows the search for possible solutions. Suggested solutions are tested and appraised as to their practicality and desirability in an effort to find the best solution. If one can be found, arguments are advanced and appeals are designed for its approval. However, we should point out that in this world of imperfection and human frailties, not all problems can be resolved by some simple plan of action. Some problems are to be lived with, but lived with in the light of some adjustments and revised interpretations and value judgments. Thus, in some instances, constructive ideas which have solution value may be integrated with the need picture. The urgency of the need diminishes by means of reasoned discourse which modifies meaning, mood, and attitudes concerning certain concepts. The solution concept may therefore in some instances be a relative term including ideas dealing with interpretations or evaluations which help the listener adopt new points of view and modify his appreciation of the nature of the problem and how to live with it.

6. *The Compelling Order*

The compelling order is the most complex and challenging of all. It requires careful thought, detailed planning, a sense of the dramatic, an understanding of human nature, and a grasp of the basic laws which govern audience psychology. The compelling order embraces a method which is more psychological than logical. The pattern of arrangement becomes more of an art and less of a science. Intangible factors are given greater consideration—such factors as interest, attention, suggestion, and motivational appeals. The goal is to gather increased strength for an idea by a rising level of listener concern for it.

The larger concept of the compelling order may be broken down into a variety of patterns. But our field here is too broad and extensive to give it fullest coverage. We confine our attention, therefore, to the following:

a. *The build-up.* Here the law of climax prevails. The speaker arranges his ideas and formulates his phrases and sentences with the view of gaining momentum in attaining audience interest. He gets the snowball effect, as is demonstrated in Mark Antony's speech in *Julius Caesar,* which is an excellent example of accumulation of force and dramatic interest. Study this speech carefully and note how Antony saves his prize pieces of evidence, Caesar's wounds and Caesar's will, for last.

The country minister used to say "Begin low, advance slow, rise higher, strike fire, then retire." This build-up, of course, can be greatly augmented by the speaker's manner of delivery. In a dramatic stage performance, skilled actors are able to heighten the dramatic effect of an otherwise weak climax as written by the playwright. The orator, in like manner, may do much by voice and action to lift his ideas to a higher peak of eloquence.

Some of the more common devices for the build-up include the use of suspense, repetition, rhythm, and dramatic stories. The orator may increase the number of interest elements by the use of striking facts and incidents interspersed wth well-placed phrases which crystallize his thought and drive home his message. The examples of stirring climaxes on the American platform are numerous. We mention a few—Patrick Henry's "Liberty or Death," William Jennings Bryan's "Cross of Gold," and Daniel Webster's "Liberty and Union, Now and Forever, One and Inseparable."

The climax must be firmly interwoven with the whole speech. Preparing the climax is only one phase of organization, but an important one, and it frequently strikes the balance between the success and failure of the oration.

b. *The extended story.* Put your ideas into story form. The narrative structure may supply evidence or dramatic interest, or both. The story may be fact or fiction. The story has been used ever since man could talk. Imagine the wide use of legends and stories which were handed down by word of mouth from generation to generation before the invention of the printing press. Man is by nature picture-minded. The codes of human conduct and the laws for orderly living are instilled in us from childhood in story form. Our destiny is shaped, in part, at our mother's knee by nursery rhymes, Bible stories, and folklore, and, remember, adults like stories as well as children.

Janice Woelfle (Part III—"What Freedom Means to Me") employs an extended factual story as her entire long introduction. In contrast, Patricia Ann Turner ("The Constitution—Temple of Liberty") opens her oration with a fable. And Stephen Alan Oxman ("A List") tells part of the story of the debate over ratification of the Constitution and adoption of the Bill of Rights.

CHAPTER 7

Language in the Oration

LANGUAGE IN EVERYDAY LIFE

Language, in many respects, is synonymous with human progress. Ideas are communicated from one mind to another and from one generation to the next through the medium of words. Words help link the past with the present. "Words are the only things that last forever," said William Hazlitt.

We literally live in a sea of words. We are bombarded almost every hour of the day by words. We engage in conversation, answer telephone calls, listen to radio, view television, read newspapers and books, confront billboards, salesmen, and advertisements. We may hear, speak, or read twenty thousand or more words in a single day and think nothing of it. Words are almost as common as the weather, yet as vital to us as the food we eat. Words profoundly involve us in life and living. They make us happy and sad, bind us to contracts, obligate us to action, cause us to worry ourselves sick, and generally bring us success or failure. Words help create and maintain the great institutions of our free society, the home, the school, the church, the government, the marketplace. How to live without words is unimaginable.

Words may serve many functions. We may use words when in the company of others to make ourselves feel more comfortable. Words help us as we reach for a feeling of social balance and attain a sense of personal equilibrium. Little children wriggle and squirm about to be more at ease, while grownups tend to use words for the same purpose. At other times we use words with little or no effort as we engage in idle conversation and participate in nonsensical chatter. They help us, so to speak, in our mental doodling. As our purpose becomes more definite and particular wants emerge more clearly, we use words for routine matters such as ordering groceries, going shopping, filling the gas tank of the family car, playing games, and so on. As we are mentally challenged to express our opinions and make value judgments about social, religious, economic, political, or moral questions, we give more thought to the words we use. And as our personal convictions become involved, we at times may use language which is more expressive of ourselves; that is to say, we use words and phrases which reflect characteristics of our personality. Our friends may say, "That sounds just like you." Some people, as they become excited and emotionally aroused, tend to use stronger language and even become careless and use words with excessive emotional force, words that carry extra voltage such as "thief," "liar," "crook," "snob," "slacker," "slut," "hood," "Communist," "traitor," "coward," and the like. Such words laden with emotion often cloud the real meaning and become barriers to communication of the intended meaning. But the language which concerns us most as orators is that which grows out of sincere thought and feeling and reflects beauty, clarity, force, and imagination. In simple terms, we are interested in language which appeals, at least to some degree, to the listener's literary sense. Here is where the orator comes into the picture. The characteristics of this kind of language are the main concern of this chapter; however, before we turn our attention to the role of language in the oration, it is important to have an understanding of some of the essential differences between spoken and written language.

SPOKEN AND WRITTEN LANGUAGE COMPARED

Eye and ear appeal. The written word is for the eye, the spoken word is for the ear. The organs of sight and hearing have widely differing sensory functions. What we see makes an instantaneous photographic impression upon the mind which, in essence, is intellectual. What we hear tends to be more emotional in character. To see is to believe, to hear is to get excited. Thus stated, the point is somewhat oversimplified, yet there is much truth in it; hence, music is the most emotional of all arts. We may spend dollars by stuffing dimes into juke boxes and spend a quarter only once or twice in a lifetime to attend art museums. There is an old saying, "You can't fight a war without a drum," and centuries ago the English playwright William Congreve wrote, "Music hath charms to soothe the savage breast." The magic that lies in ear appeal explains why most of us find it more exciting to listen to newscasters than to read the same news in the morning paper, and why it is more impressive to listen to a speech over radio or television than it is to read the same speech in the newspapers.

Here lies, in part, the clue to the hidden power of oratory.

The printed word carries the image of authority. We tend to believe more readily what we see in print than what we hear. The spoken word seems to be elusive, difficult to pin down; hence, written documents and signed confessions become binding before the law. If someone doubts our word, we say, "See for yourself; it's in the book." The spoken word runs the risk of being changed or altered or misquoted by the listener, but the written word stands for all to see, and it is not to be tampered with.

The speaker and writer start at different poles. The speaker has a flesh-and-blood audience before him—he stands before his listeners in person and knows almost exactly to whom he is talking and how his message is being received, but the writer knows little or nothing about his readers or how they will react to his ideas. Thus, the speaker and writer start off with widely different attitudes. Once the writer has put his ideas on paper for his readers to see, he in effect surrenders control of his product. It is like mailing a letter—once it is dropped into the slot in the mailbox, it is gone beyond recall. The speaker, on the other hand (unless he is speaking for radio or television), can revise the substance of his speech, modify his meaning by gestures, posture, vocal inflection, and even is free to modify his language during the progress of his speech.

Written and oral style compared. Most readers can read two to four times faster than they normally speak, even if the vocabulary is more difficult. The speaker's vocabulary is smaller and more limited than the writer's. The reader can pause and recheck the meaning of words; this the listener cannot do. Speaking or listening is a one-shot affair. The speaker must be more careful, therefore, to use words that are instantly understood. His words must be simple, short, direct, more personal at times, and his imagery sharp and clear. He should also favor words of Anglo-Saxon origin and use many short, simple, direct, declarative sentences. The language style of your oration is not, as some people seem to think, the same as that of your written theme in an English course. An oration must never be, as one famous speech professor put it, "an essay standing on its hind legs."

Although there may be fundamental differences in language style for speaking and writing, there are many characteristics common to both forms of discourse. Speaking and writing are not totally separate means to separate ends. Both written and spoken words are tools for thinking; each mode of language use is helpful to the other in expressing ideas. The orator must therefore learn how to think with paper and pencil. He must first put his tongue-born words on paper. He must, so to speak, engage in conversation in ink. This is a training step for his eventual confrontation with a live audience. Thus writing helps to get your mind in gear, helps to select your words with care. Only by writing can you get a working blueprint from which you can construct your thoughts, refine them, and compose the unified total product. Writing serves as a means for formulating and creating your most effective oral style.

LANGUAGE IN THE ORATION

LANGUAGE IN YOUR ORATION

Language in your oration is the crux of this chapter. Obviously we are not thinking merely of words as such, but words grouped in phrases, sentences, paragraphs, and the composition of words in their entirety as they concern the unified, completed speech. We might make a variety of approaches to the functions of language in your oration. Partly for the sake of efficiency and partly in the interest of clarity, we have chosen to develop the concepts around the four traditional characteristics of effective language in the oration. They are: clarity, correctness, appropriateness, and impressiveness. Around this format we will present the essential considerations of language in your oration.

CLARITY

See to it that your words make sense. A speaker can put a lot of words together which sound eloquent, yet make little or no sense. Here is an example of a part of a speech which has nice-sounding phrases and some hints of ideas, but in which real thought substance never emerges.

It is indeed an honor and a privilege for me to speak on a subject of such great importance. As I ponder this question, I am filled with inspiration. I sincerely hope that you who cherish liberty and freedom will exercise your God-given rights and rally to this noble cause and find a solution, a solution which will assure peace with honor. Seldom in the course of human affairs have we faced so great a responsibility, seldom have we had a more glorious opportunity to stand up for what is right. I am sure you will reap the rewards of happiness as you carry out your individual duty in this worthy endeavor.

May the light of truth guide your conscience, and may I say again, it is the past that lies behind us; it is the present that is here with us now; and it is the future that lies before us.

This may sound lofty and noble, but it says nothing. It doesn't make sense. Words! Words! Words!

Use simple words. Big words do not necessarily express big ideas. The Bible is written in simple language. The Twenty-third Psalm has 118 words, 92 of which are of one syllable. Many of Shakespeare's finest passages are filled with simple words. In Hamlet's most famous soliloquy, 99 out of 118 words are of one syllable. The first words are: "To be or not to be . . . ." Winston Churchill paid tribute to the Royal Air Force by saying, "Never in the field of human conflict was so much owed by so many to so few." Abraham Lincoln said, "This government cannot endure permanently half slave and half free." Simple words make the meaning clear. Involved phraseology saps the vitality from what the orator says and makes it doubly difficult for the listener. Simplicity leads to understanding, and understanding is the touchstone of conviction and persuasion.

Use the specific and concrete. Since the terms *specific* and *concrete* have much in common, we will use them together. The opposite of *specific* is *general*. The opposite of *concrete* is *abstract*. The term *insect* is general, *grasshopper* is specific; *animal* is general, *monkey* is specific. If you say you are "homesick," you are using an abstract term; if you say you are "longing to put your feet under the family table and have a piece of the juicy hot apple pie Mother makes," you are more concrete. If you write home and ask your father to please send money, you are very general; but if you say "Please send $25; I need $19.50 for books and $4.20 for library fees," you are getting down to specifics.

Use precise and accurate terms. Precision and accuracy should not be confused with the specific and concrete. We are here concerned with terms which convey meaning which is more definite and more nearly correct. Such terms as *few, many, big, afraid, industrious* need further explanation to express more accurately the intended meaning. When Franklin D. Roosevelt said, "I see one-third of a nation ill-housed, ill-clad, and ill-nourished," he was more accurate than if he had said, "There is poverty in the land." It is more accurate to say, "The star center on the basketball team is six feet nine inches tall, weighing 230 pounds" than to say, "The star center is a big man."

CORRECTNESS

Correctness here refers to the prescribed, standard rules of correct usage in matters of grammar and pronunciation. If we consider writing, then spelling and punctuation should be included. Grammatical soundness is more important in oratory than in debate and extempore speaking, for the orator has ample opportunity to refine his phrasing and sentence structure to conform with the rules of grammar and English usage. Since you may have many rehearsals of your oration, noticeable errors in pronunciation should also be corrected. Obvious and frequent errors in grammar and pronunciation will be heavily penalized by your judges.

BUILDING THE CONTEST ORATION

An oration is an excellent means for teaching the habits of good grammar and acceptable pronunciation.

APPROPRIATENESS

The goal of appropriateness of the language in your oration concerns what is fitting and in good taste. Language which is appropriate may be considered from three points of view, namely: what is in good taste and suitable to you, the orator; what is suitable to the meaning and mood you wish to convey; and what is suitable to the situation, the audience, and the occasion.

Language should fit the orator. The language should, in a sense, sound like you. Language is sometimes referred to as "dress for the thought." It also serves, to a degree, to give the listener an impression of the kind of person you are. It should therefore be fitting and in good taste to reflect your unique individuality. You wouldn't expect a five-year-old child to sound like an old man. Neither would you expect the language of an adult to sound like that of a second grader.

The style of the male orator would be different from that of the female orator. Experienced English teachers, when reading unsigned essays or themes, can usually tell if they are written by a boy or a girl. No ghost writer should write your oration. Use the language, therefore, most becoming and best suited to express your maturity of mind, your judgment, your sex, your creative imagination, and yourself. This helps you to be natural, genuine, and sincere.

Language should be suitable to the subject. Language should also serve to convey the thought and emotion accurately, clearly, and with fidelity. The speaker who seeks to attain this goal by the use of words needs to pay attention to words which are fitting and becoming to the meaning and mood. We have all noted the difference in language of television commercials designed to sell dog foods or pianos, liver pills or life insurance. Language which develops the mood or substance of a sermon in the pulpit will probably be very different from that used by the man who lectures on pest control.

The architect selects stones and materials which are appropriate and fitting for what he is constructing, be it a retaining wall, a residence, or a cathedral. Although some stones and mortar used to build a sidewalk may be the same as those used for a cathedral, it is the way the stones are fitted together and arranged that makes the structure effective. In the same way, the orator may use many of the same words used at home, at school, or at play, but it is the way they are fitted together to suit the thought which determines their effectiveness.

Language should fit the audience and the occasion. Language which suits the speaker and his subject must also be suited to the audience and occasion. Fortunately for most high school orators, the audience is usually composed of students, parents, teachers, and friends, who listen with a favorable attitude. When speaking over the radio or for television, the audience is more general, less selective, but still largely a neutral or friendly one. We may be generalizing a bit, but it seems reasonable to assume your audience will be above average in intelligence, above average in its educational background, and more sympathetic than hostile. The occasion will also be more formal than informal, the tone of the meeting more dignified than casual, and the purpose of the meeting more specific than general.

People generally tend to modify their language when they talk to each other in accordance with the environment and the purpose of the occasion. Language heard on the playground would probably be quite different from that heard in the principal's office, and the casual chitchat with your friends seated on stools, drinking cokes at the drugstore soda fountain, would not be the same as that heard at the annual Senior Honors Banquet. We tend to suit our language to our listeners and the occasion in everyday life; we should make a special effort to do the same in contest oratory.

IMPRESSIVENESS

In the first chapter we pointed out that oratory should be made to stand out over ordinary speech. The ancient Greeks looked upon oratory as the aristocrat of all forms of public speaking. The stature of an oration usually depends upon the quality of its language. The more creative aspects of the oration often show best in its literary tone. This is the *touchstone* of language in oratory.

What are some of the characteristics of the literary tone or the impressive qualities of language in the oration? It is difficult to compose a complete inventory of such characteristics and vividly describe them. For our purpose, we have selected five important elements or characteristics for your study and consideration: imagery, originality, dignity, beauty, and force. These qualities do not necessarily stand out apart from each other as separate entities. They are blended and integrated to produce a composite effect, yet each quality plays a role which can be identified as it contributes to the total communication impact.

Imagery. Imagery is the mainstay of poetry. Its role is also most important in oratory. The chief function of imagery is to visualize the ideas, to flash a mental picture before the listener's mind. In addition to being an aid to clarity, it also serves to glorify and ennoble thoughts and feelings and intensify them. It often lifts the idea above the level of the commonplace. Its values in oratory are many, but perhaps chief among them is the power to make a vital, central idea simple, impressive, and at times dramatic. Certain political figures are often long remembered thanks to an image created of them by means of oratory. Robert Ingersoll won oratorical fame for his nomination speech of Colonel James G. Blaine for President when he called him "the plumed knight." In like manner, Franklin D. Roosevelt became better known after his nominating speech of Al Smith, whom he symbolized as "the happy warrior." Many issues and causes are often remembered through oratorical images. The initial title or subject of some speeches may fade from public memory while the key image of the speech remains. Churchill's "Iron Curtain" speech, Franklin D. Roosevelt's "Stab in the Back" speech, Bryan's "Cross of Gold" speech, Lincoln's "House Divided" speech, Patrick Henry's "Liberty or Death" speech are examples of sharp, effective imagery which stand out like bright stars in the oratorical firmament.

The most common and useful types of images are simile, metaphor, and personification. A *simile* compares two things, using the word *as* or *like*. For instance, "The woman chattered like a magpie" is a simile, but "She is a magpie" is a *metaphor*. In Carl Sandburg's poem "Fog" the sentence "The fog comes on little cat feet" is a metaphor. The metaphor likens two things or concepts more closely without the use of the comparative word *as* or *like*. When Churchill said, "An *iron curtain* has descended across the Continent," he used a metaphor.

Personification is a way of attributing personal traits to inanimate objects and abstract ideas: "My old car groaned and coughed and shivered with cold"; "The sun smiled on us"; "The wind whispered in our ears." These are examples of personification.

Now a word of caution and advice. Imagery must be used with taste and discretion. It is easy for the young, imaginative mind to get carried away from the main line of thought by the lure of impressive word imagery. You must never let the impressiveness of your language overshadow the true meaning. Ornamentation should add to the beauty and force of what you have to say, not detract from it. A discriminating use of ornamentation has its place in an oration, but too much of it can destroy the impact of your speech. A young lady at a formal party, overdressed in loud, gaudy colors, may succeed only in being most conspicuous, while detracting from the natural beauty and charm which she seeks to enhance.

Originality. Originality is the quality of being creative in thought, language, and delivery in a unique, individual way. To be original is to produce something distinctive of your own, something that is not copied or imitated. The claim of personal authorship and the stamp of individuality is our concern here. Obviously, thought, language, and delivery must be integrated in your oration, but the attention of the audience is focused upon originality of word expression and language style. The language should be your own: your phrasing, choice of words, and the application of those words to represent the product of your thinking and feeling. One good way to be original is to avoid trite, overworked words and commonplace expressions as much as you can. Clothing worn again and again on repeated occasions soon becomes worn and tiresome. Make a list of the threadbare expressions that pop up in your mind in the early stages of preparing your oration. You may come face to face with such expressions as "it gives me great pleasure," "according to statistics," "best authorities say," "beyond a shadow of a doubt," "last but not least," "now in conclusion," and so on. Threadbare and overused adjectives are more common, such as "terrific," "great," "swell," "fabulous," "cute," "marvelous," and the like. Avoid worn and trite words and expressions as much as possible.

Dignity, beauty, force. These three qualities interact upon one another. We will focus our attention largely upon *dignity,* assuming that if dignity is achieved, the desired beauty and force will often be the byproducts. Dignified language enlists the admiration and respect of the audience. Dignity is the opposite of casualness, cheapness, colloquialisms, and matter-of-factness. Dignity suggests a degree of formality, propriety; it suggests style and distinction. A dignified tone of language gives an edge of importance to what you say and adds tone to the occasion in general. Dignity does not mean stiffness or stuffiness; neither does it suggest a cold, austere, and impersonal tone. The quality of dignity stands out in great literature such as the Bible and Shakespeare. Dignity of language is an outstanding quality in the oratory of Daniel Webster, Abraham Lincoln, Winston Churchill, Adlai E. Stevenson, and in some addresses by the late President John F. Kennedy.

Dignity is often heightened or reinforced by appropriate imagery. Observe how Shakespeare attained a fine literary tone by skillfully blending poignant imagery in the speech of Horatio in the death scene of his friend Hamlet:

> Now cracks a noble heart. Goodnight, sweet prince,
> And flights of angels sing thee to thy rest.

Here is great dignity, beauty, and power. We might paraphrase these lines into the vernacular, commonplace language in this manner:

> Heaven's sakes, my buddy has kicked off!
> He was a mighty good fellow. May his soul be saved.

The contrast between the literary tone created by Shakespeare and the practical, prosaic vernacular is shockingly crude and appalling.

Perhaps one good way to impress upon us the value of dignity and literary tone of language would be recasting the essential meanings of Lincoln's Gettysburg Address in an extremely folksy, casual style. We might start off something like this: "A little more than eighty years ago our great-grandfathers started a new country. They had the notion that everybody should have a fair chance and that no one should have the jump on the other fellow, just because of birth."

These two above examples show how factual matter may be expressed in radically different ways by the medium of language. The literary tone has power, beauty, dignity. Our imaginations are kindled by it to fill in extra meanings and emotions. It stirs us to bring forth the better side of our nature, and such is the mission of oratory.

ADDITIONAL LANGUAGE DEVICES TO MAKE IDEAS IMPRESSIVE

Use rhetorical questions. The rhetorical question is one which gives the listener a mental burden. He is challenged to ponder a point. You drop an idea, so to speak, in his lap and prod him to think and act. The speaker does not answer the question directly, although he may guide and prod the listener to the answer he wants. This is one of the most effective standard devices of oratory. Patrick Henry, as noted in Chapter 5, used rhetorical questions to accumulate force in his famous speech on liberty:

They tell us, sir, that we are weak; unable to cope with so formidable an adversary. But when shall we be stronger?

Will it be the next week, or the next year? Will it be when we are totally disarmed, and when a British guard shall be stationed in every house? Shall we gather strength by irresolution and inaction? Shall we acquire the means of effectual resistance by lying supinely on our backs, and hugging the delusive phantom of hope, until our enemies shall have bound us hand and foot? Sir, we are not weak, if we make proper use of the means which the God of nature hath placed in our power.

Ask leading questions and answer them. This device may be geared more for clarity than for impressiveness, yet it often lends itself to making a point stick in the mind of the listener. Children drive their parents to distraction with a barrage of questions. This is natural, for questions are the stepping stones to learning. Asking questions was the favorite device of the Greek philosopher Socrates (hence the expression "the Socratic method"). It is a commonly used method found in news magazines and on some of the editorial pages of our newspapers. Note how one speaker, talking about the use of electricity in the home, asked a question, then answered it: "What do we mean by a 'kilowatt hour'? A kilowatt hour is a unit by which electric energy is measured, just as the bushel is the unit for measuring wheat and corn, the gallon the unit for measuring gasoline, and the pound the unit for measuring butter. For example, one fifty-watt light burning for twenty hours will use one kilowatt-hour of electricity."

Jesus asked the question, "Who is my neighbor?" Then he answered his own question with the parable of the Good Samaritan.

Use repetition and refrain. This device has already been discussed in Chapter 5. We merely call attention

118

to it here. It, too, helps to impress basic ideas on the audience's mind. But remember that the overuse of repetition may lead to triteness and boredom.

Use colorful words and phrases. This is a broad category, and we have touched upon it in various ways before. Some words and phrases carry extra power and have implied meanings which intensify the listener's emotional response. The orator usually has a choice of words by which meanings may be brought out more vividly and more impressively. For instance, the words *hand* and *claw, spit* and *expectorate, work* and *labor, sweat* and *perspire, fire* and *discharge, die* and *expire, unemployed* and *jobless, wealthy* and *rich, ignorant* and *uninformed* may have similar dictionary definitions yet have widely different meanings in an oration. To say "I am broke" may be more effective than to say "I am out of money." "Go see a doctor" is stronger than "I think you should consult a physician." "Yankee go home" is more colorful than "Foreigners are not wanted on our shores."

Consider when you may use strong nouns, adjectives, and verbs. For instance, *clasp* seems more strong and colorful than *hold*. It seems more effective to say, "He stalked out of the meeting," than to say, "He left before the meeting was over." Of course, as the orator seeks and selects words and phrases to give color and force to his thoughts, he must not offend his audience; he must be sensitive to the standards of good taste and abide by them.

CHAPTER 8

Delivery

Unique and Dynamic Aspects of Delivery

Delivery makes the oration a reality. Delivery is that part of the process whereby the oration becomes an accomplished fact. You are not an experienced orator until you have delivered your oration. Your greatest thrill and your most enduring satisfaction comes from your experience in delivering your speech before judges and audience.

Delivery reinforces and energizes the basic ideas. The *prime function* of delivery is to act as an effective agent for bringing forth the substance of the oration in a compelling manner. It does more than merely project the subject matter for listener comprehension. Delivery can be a powerful lever for lifting thought and emotion far above the ordinary level of requirements for being heard and understood. It puts voltage into your meaning. By voice and action, the orator can give added beauty to words and phrases and generally make his ideas more appealing, more dramatic, and more forceful. To the degree that any aspect of vocal or bodily delivery reinforces the meaning or idea you are trying to communicate, to that degree it represents good delivery. When delivery detracts or distracts from meaning it becomes ineffective.

DELIVERY

Delivery brings forth your image as a person and an orator. A new kind of intimacy emerges between you and your listeners. As you deliver your speech, the audience forms its impressions of you, good or bad. As it gets to know you, it sizes you up from a thousand clues as to your character, your knowledge of the subject, your intelligence, the worthiness of your ideas, your mastery of self and occasion, your earnestness of purpose and nobility of intent.

Delivery helps speaker and audience to function as a team. You and your audience are not separate and distinct parts, detached from one another. You are of one and the same crew. The listeners want you to succeed, even though they may not agree with what you say. They nevertheless rejoice in your triumphs and cheer your best efforts. They tend to react in empathy with your language, your bodily action, and your vocal expressions. The team spirit is there. It is an important asset in your speech. Capitalize on it as you act your part as leader of the team.

Beware—the dual role of delivery. Like a double-edged sword, delivery can cut both ways. It can serve as a positive, constructive force on the one hand, while on the other hand it has veto power and can spoil what otherwise would be a good speech. Poor delivery inflicts a heavy penalty on both speaker and speech. A most carefully prepared speech, rich in substance, well structured and well phrased, can fail if the delivery is dull and boring. Experienced judges of contest oratory frequently are heard to say, "What a pity that John was so poor in delivery! I would have ranked him first but for that."

Important as delivery is in oratory, we must realize that it remains a supplementary agent and that by itself it does not make a speech. However, excellence in delivery is almost indispensable for high-grade oratorical performance.

Delivery is that part of speaking which can best be rehearsed. Content, organization, and language are aspects of speaking which do not lend themselves to rehearsal as delivery does. However, delivery rehearsal can help toward improvement in the use of supporting materials, orderly arrangement of thought, and language expression. Delivery rehearsals help to test out and refine the entire speaking process and thus bring the oratorical performance to a higher pitch of effectiveness.

Practice should be of the right type and right amount. The old adage, "Practice makes perfect," does not always hold true when it comes to oratory. Practice doesn't make perfect; only *perfect* practice makes perfect. Continued haphazard and aimless delivery rehearsals may be worse than no rehearsals at all. The wrong kind of practice will only make bad habits more permanent; therefore, practice in delivery should be carried out carefully and purposefully. Aim to reach a point in your rehearsals where you are so familiar with your speech that you can completely throw yourself into it and thus lose yourself in what you say. Then you won't worry about *how* to say it. Your thought and purpose should command *you* in your delivery. Here is the secret of self-command, of sincerity, spontaneity, fluency, and enthusiasm.

GUIDES TO EFFECTIVE DELIVERY

Develop the intensified, animated conversational mode. The modern style of speech delivery is very different from that of a half century ago. Speakers today are more of this world, more earthbound, more direct, more human, more natural, and more conversational than speakers of bygone years. There is less of the studied elocutionary style, less showmanship, less exhibitionism, and more of the communicative spirit which reflects the "you-and-I" attitude. The orator of today does not stand on a pedestal and strike a pose to impress his admiring listeners. He does not stand apart from them; he is one of them. He talks *with* his hearers, not *at* them; he shares ideas with them instead of hurling ideas at them.

Although the modern speaker may appear more casual and informal than the orators of old, this does not mean he is less forceful. He simply puts less stock in sound and fury and table-pounding to gain his communication impact and puts more faith in meaning and in the cooperative attitude of his audience. But the "conversational mode" of delivery does not mean sloppy, overly informal, inarticulate vocal and physical delivery. Oratorical delivery should strive for the intensified, animated conversational style. This mode of speech is most becoming, most flexible, and lends itself best to pleasing oral presentation.

BUILDING THE CONTEST ORATION

Be sincere. The oration must ring true. Counterfeit coins are detected by their artificial ring. We may not all be able to be artistic or clever, but we can all be sincere. Insincerity is one of the last things an audience or judge will forgive in a speaker. Integrity and honesty are the twin virtues of sincerity; they are the opposite of sham and hypocrisy. Honesty was part of the secret of Abraham Lincoln's eloquence. Sincerity, claimed John Quincy Adams, is the "first principle of political oratory."

Be enthusiastic. Emerson once said, "Nothing great was ever achieved without enthusiasm." Enthusiasm is sometimes described as "the human spirit on fire." It is something we see in the eyes of children when they think of Santa Claus at Christmas time. It is something which Tiny Tim had in Dickens' *Christmas Carol.* It is contagious and spreads like a prairie fire. It is a priceless virtue of the orator, and to the listener it has irresistible appeal.

Make your ideas sound important. Nothing is so deadening as an overcasual "I don't care" attitude. No matter how small the audience, never permit your role as a speaker to sink to the cheap, commonplace level. President Theodore Roosevelt, who had a rather high-pitched, unpleasant voice, gained the reputation of being a very forceful and dynamic speaker. He always observed one simple rule: make it sound important. No matter what the occasion, he spoke as though everything he said was of utmost importance and every word was deserving of the listeners' respectful attention. He acted the part of the man who cared. He had mastered the secret of making everything he said seem very important. Of course it is necessary that what you say not only sound important but also actually *be* important.

Wrap yourself around your speech. The most compelling force which reacts upon others is the human personality. Your total self composed of your character, your ideas, your appearance, your attitude, your hopes and fears cannot be completely detached from your speaking. The real "you" offers a source of eloquence which is individual and unique. No art is so completely bound up with the self as is that of speech. In his *Rhetoric,* Aristotle maintained that the orator's "character may almost be called the most effective means of persuasion he possesses." Those attributes of temperament, friendliness, courage, and so forth reflected in your talk are assets which you should put to good use. They help create an image of authority in the minds of the listeners. Dare to be yourself. Ralph Waldo Emerson believed, "What you are stands over you . . . and thunders so that I cannot hear what you say to the contrary."

Be the thirteenth man on the jury. Daniel Webster, one of the greatest American orators of all time, knew the importance of communication for a speaker. In one of his famous court trials, the jury, having received its instructions from the judge, retired to an adjoining room for its deliberations. The foreman of the jury turned to the group and said, "Gentlemen, it seems as though Mr. Webster is in this room with us as the thirteenth man of the jury, trying to decide this case." Webster had so completely projected his ideas and his personality to the jury that he literally seemed to become one of them. He shared his ideas, feelings, and himself on a common-ground basis. He made the jury feel he was one of them. He had the communicative spirit.

COMMUNICATION IMPACT THROUGH THE EYES OF THE LISTENER

Bodily action is a code for meaning. The orator is seen as well as heard. The visual aspects of delivery include all possible bodily movements, walking, gestures, facial expressions, posture, eye contact, head movements, dress, and so on. We must accept the fact that we do talk with our bodies, and bodily action is a salient part of delivery, providing an inescapable code for conveying ideas and feelings. Of course, not all bodily movements have a direct bearing upon the communication of the speech substance. Some bodily movements simply help release tensions of the speaker and give him the feeling of comfort and ease. They indicate that he is reaching for some kind of personal equilibrium.

"What should I do with my hands?" is an expression often heard among the oratorical fledglings, and the teacher usually says, "Forget them." But the solution of the problem is not that simple. The idea is to get so absorbed in more important matters that what you do with your hands does not matter. Put your whole mind on what you say and become genuinely involved in sharing your ideas and yourself with your listeners. In other words, lose yourself in your speech, and your hands won't get in your way. Take comfort in the thought that you have hands and that they will take care of themselves if you take care of the main business, namely, your central purpose and the central idea of your speech. Why not spend less time worrying about your hands and more time thinking about your message? Why not thank Heaven you have hands? They are among your most expressive agents and are a source of security. Imagine having to make a speech in a strait-jacket! It is a good feeling to know that you have hands which are free and ready to come to your rescue should you need them.

Be grateful that you don't have to worry about studied, mechanical bodily movements. Be glad that bodily action is natural for the communication of ideas. Take a reassuring lesson from children as you watch them at play. Observe how they use their hands, faces, feet, heads, eyes, and so forth, as they laugh and chatter at play.

Note the many ways in which bodily action can help you. It can help you release tensions and be more re-laxed; it can help free your mind and thus speed up the mental processes; it helps enlist the attention and in-terest of the audience; it helps to bring out your per-sonality and reflect the sincerity of your purpose. It generally adds life and tone to your delivery.

The single greatest and most important function of action is to reveal and reinforce the meaning. In this sense, gestures and bodily action have a fourfold mis-sion:

1. They punctuate ideas and emphasize them. The writer uses punctuation marks and capital letters to emphasize thought and shade his meanings. The writer is governed by rules; the speaker is not. The emphatic gestures follow no set pattern.

2. Gestures help make ideas clear. Descriptive gestures show relationships in both space and time. They may indicate direction, distance, and shapes. Even past time may be suggested by bodily attitude and the backward glance of the eyes, while the tomorrows may be indicated by forward or upward bodily attitudes and eye glances. A great variety of bodily expressions can be effective in narration and description. For instance, an exciting episode or a dramatic moment in a sporting event might be ridiculously dull and even humorously unconvincing when told without the slightest hint of bodily expression.

3. Action and gesture reflect personal feelings and attitudes. Have you ever watched a hungry lad bite into a juicy peach and see satisfied expression in his face? If the peach were sour or bitter, his face and bodily reaction would be quite different. Shaking and nodding of the head are gestures of approval or disapproval. Gestures revealing personal attitudes have a wide range and usually come quite naturally.

4. Gestures help to dramatize ideas. Dramatic gestures are symbolic of added excitement and the importance of thought. They are usually more subtle than the purely emphatic or descriptive gesture. They usually call special attention to a point in your speech

before it is made. An outstretched arm and hand of the minister when giving the benediction, or the sharp clap of the hands by a speaker before making a point, or the snapping of fingers by the kindergarten teacher are examples of the dramatic gesture. Dramatic gestures, when properly used, can be very effective, but they should be used with discretion and used sparingly.

We will now list some specific suggestions for using effective gestures and bodily action:

Suit your gestures to the meaning. Action must be in harmony with the thought and feeling expressed in words. Observe the wisdom of Hamlet as he gives advice to the players, "Suit the words to the action and the action to the words." Wild, windmill-like gestures unrelated to thought look ridiculous. Don't tear "a passion to tatters."

Suit your gesture to the purpose, the occasion, and your personality. If you are in a large auditorium before a large audience, you should use more action and more gestures of the broad, sweeping type than if you are in a small room with only a handful of people. If you are the quiet, reserved type of person, you probably would not use such pronounced bodily action as that of the robust, highly mobile, athletic type of person. We expect girls to be more restrained in the use of bodily expression than boys. But generally high school orators are guiltier of using too little bodily expression than too much.

Carry out your gestures and bodily movements in a positive and wholehearted manner. Halfhearted, hesitant, and uncertain gestures indicate indecision and timidity. Often these petty little timid actions are worse than no action at all. Such meaningless visual scribblings attract attention to the speaker and interfere with the communication of his thought. Gestures should be made with assurance and determination. They should be made in a positive, wholehearted manner involving the whole physical personality. Gestures and actions of the orator should not resemble those of a puppet. It is not a matter of a finger or a hand or an arm, but usually a matter of the whole body from the toes to the top of the head. They should be made with *definiteness* and *completeness*. They should be sharp and clean-cut. There should be no doubt in the listener's mind as to the meaning a specific action or gesture is intended to convey.

Posture and platform appearance are important. The audience is quick to form an impression of you as a speaker by your posture and appearance. Posture is a subtle factor and tends to create an image of the speaker which lingers long in the minds of the audience.

When we think about posture, we consider more than just the speaker's stance. The speaker is more than a statue; he is a living personality in action. We sense the fuller meaning of posture as we observe the tennis player or basketball player on the courts, poised for action. We become aware of the attributes of poise, grace, balance, and complete bodily coordination. Plato wrote about posture, "The beautiful motion is that which produces the desired result with the least effort." It is important that you, the orator, look the part; that is to say, it is important that you create the impression that you are at your best and ready to do your best with ease.

Consider a few suggestions for effective posture and appearance. It is important that you cultivate the attitude of tallness. Think tall, stand tall, and talk tall. This attitude will help avoid a sloppy, droopy, negative look. Try to appear relaxed, yet be on your mental toes, poised for action. Assume the attitude of being purposeful and businesslike, yet don't look too austere or severe; reflect the spirit of friendly dignity.

Communication Impact Through the Ears of the Listener

Speeches are made essentially to be heard; while bodily action may reinforce and amplify meaning and serve as an aid to clarity, it is the voice which does most to dramatize, emotionalize, and emphasize ideas. Seeing is believing, while hearing is more a matter of feeling. We might say your ears and heart are close together. Music is often called the most emotional of all arts. Music is a psychological weapon in warfare. It has been said that Napoleon was a master on the field of battle because he never taught his drummer boys how to beat a retreat. They were experts only at beating a charge.

The voice carries the magic touch that stirs the souls of men. The three main functions of the orator's voice are to reinforce and heighten the meaning, to create and individualize the speaker's image, and to emotionalize and dramatize what the speaker says.

131

BUILDING THE CONTEST ORATION

There are three basic standards for effective vocal delivery: (1) the speaker must be heard; (2) the speaker must be understood; and (3) the speaker must be pleasing. The speaker who clearly fails to meet any one of these three standards fails in his role as an effective oral communicator.

We will now list a number of specific points which are significant in most listeners' scale of values:

Listeners like a voice with adequate force and energy. The listener's first right is to hear the speaker without undue strain or effort. The listener should not be made to feel that he must turn his head or cup his hand behind his ear or strain every nerve to hear the speaker. The other extreme is that of the loud, powerful, booming voice turned on full blast in a tiny room before a half dozen people. This may be as bad as not being able to hear the speaker at all. However, this is exceptional. The weak, low-volume voice is much more common than the one which needs to be tuned down.

Listeners like a voice with a pure, clear tone. The voice should be free from harshness, fuzziness, or huskiness. It should not sound hard or have a metallic tone or reflect an unpleasant, high, nasal pitch. The voice should have a firm, resonant quality which is the touchstone of vocal purity.

Listeners like to hear distinct, clean-cut utterances of words and syllables. Words should fall from the lips of the speaker clearly and distinctly like newly minted coins. The real cause of slovenly diction is carelessness. We develop lazy lips and a lazy tongue, and the laziness in the use of these organs causes us to slur the consonant sounds and run them together, thus making us guilty of mumbling.

Listeners like vocal expression with variety and color. Nothing is duller than a speaker who drones on and on in a deadly, monotonous tone of voice. Vocal variety may be gained by variation in pitch, rate, and force. However, variety in pitch is usually the key for developing vocal variety.

Listeners like fluency in speech delivery. Fluency should not be confused with glibness or merely rapid utterance. A speedy talker is not necessarily a fluent speaker. Fluency has more to do with moving the thought forward. The listeners like the speaker to keep his thoughts marching along toward the goal. They want to feel that the speaker is getting somewhere, that he is covering the ground, that they are joining him on a thought journey. Listeners resent the flow of thought that is marked by awkward pauses, with speech that is cluttered with *ah*'s and *er*'s, and where fluency is impaired by jerky stops and starts.

Listeners like to be thought-conscious, not word-conscious. The listener prefers to be involved in thought and feeling, rather than in the language the speaker uses. Words and phrases should not stick out like a sore thumb; they should not jar the listeners' senses. The point is that ideas should come alive, not words. Therefore, in your delivery it is important to give emphasis to your thought, not your words. Think and re-live the meaning. Make the audience aware of what you say, not the language you use. Stress the thought, not the words. In his *De Oratore*, Cicero emphasized that nothing could be "so idiotic as a mere jingle of words, be they as choice and perfect as you will, if there is no meaning or knowledge underlying them."

PART III

Selected Winning Contest Orations

THE IRRESPONSIBLES

JOEL SWABB, MUSKINGUM COLLEGE

FIRST PLACE, 1963 NATIONAL FINALS, INTERSTATE
ORATORICAL ASSOCIATION CONTEST

The time is 3 A.M. The place, the home of a
Protestant minister in Phoenix, Arizona. The minister
awakens to the ringing of his telephone. He wonders
what member of his congregation is in need of his help
at this early hour. The voice on the other end of the line
is hard and determined, "Are you a Communist?"

The time is 11 A.M. A school teacher in Pittsburgh,
Pennsylvania sits behind her desk opening the morning
mail. She has just received a letter from a friend in
New York, a copy of *Time* magazine, and a plain white
mailing envelope with no return address. A quick slip
of the letter opener and she is greeted with the bright
red exclamation, "Communist."

It is now evening. The dinner plates have been removed and President Kennedy's light touch speech before the Washington Press Corps is receiving its final
ovation. In scanning the audience our eyes come to rest
upon one man who is obviously not amused. The ovation
dies and a tablemate nudges him with his elbow asking
at the same time his reaction. He replies in a method-
ical, serious tone of voice, "I regard him as a very
dangerous man."

These incidents are typical of the all-encompassing wrath of the archconservative, the far right, or as Archibald MacLeish put it, "the irresponsibles." It is not because they deplore softness toward communism that they have derived this title but because, as J. Edgar Hoover stated: "They are merely against communism without being for any positive measures to eliminate the social, political, and economic frictions which the Communists are so adroit at exploiting." I know the power of the "irresponsibles" because I have seen the disastrous effects they can bring upon an individual. The school teacher I spoke of a minute ago was my twelfth-grade Problems of Democracy teacher. One day in class, after telling us that we would be studying for the next two weeks the structure of the United Nations, she spoke on the importance of UNESCO. Within one week she began to receive threatening letters and telephone calls reminding her of the consequencs of teaching Communist propaganda. While the school board and administration sat back either too frightened or too confused to act, she lost twenty pounds and the classroom confidence that made her a good teacher. When the end of the semester came she resigned—broken and disheartened—while at the same time many members of the community began to embrace the cause of the "irresponsibles."

As I look back on this injustice I can see in somewhat clear perspective the cause of this teacher's plight. The accusations brought against her did not represent merely a basic mistrust in the United Nations. Rather they were a byproduct of a common trait that all "irresponsibles" exhibit—the tendency to see complex problems in terms of either-or choices. They demand that the West not give a single inch to communism, while on the other hand they denounce any and all practical persistence in combating it. Such action has forced William F. Buckley—a leading spokesman of conservatism in America—to say regretfully: The principal shortcoming of the "far right" is its inability to agree on what it stands for. They concur only on what they are against. In essence they place the unachievable against the unbearable and thus leave out any rational possibilities such as the school teacher placed her faith in.

But the influence of the "superpatriot" goes beyond the degradation of a school teacher in Pittsburgh, Pennsylvania. Today millions of well-meaning Americans have accepted the far-right approach as their means of coping with the problems of the complex age in which we live. Everyday people from all types of vocations and political convictions throughout the country forget their role as "responsibles" and find themselves taking that extra step to the right. What is this extra step to the right? It is a detachment from reality and the rational thinking that our democracy relies on. It is a miscarriage of patriotic fervor. It is a loss of the ability to be able to distinguish the real enemy from one's neighbor. Above all it is the search for a simple solution that does not exist.

Let us take a long look at the results which this extremism produces. In Boston, private citizen Joe Hall, who at one time exposed and crushed a Communist front organization, was heckled by a ticket taker at a John Birch meeting: "You're a dirty Communist! Go back to Russia where you belong." In a California auditorium a "superpatriot" addressed a freedom rally. Suddenly he noticed the television cameras focused in his direction. With abruptness and anger he looked into the lens and denounced the American people with these words: "I want to talk to you Marxists and traitors out there. . . . Get the message, comrade. This country's twenty-year Rip Van Winkle sleep is over."

The influence of the extremist may also be found in rural areas and secluded spots far removed from the public gaze. On a typical Sunday morning, while the mist has not yet cleared, a group of men, women, and children in a small Missouri town engage in a two-hour field drill in the problems of guerilla warfare. These minute men—with an estimated membership of 25,000 —describe themselves as "loyal American citizens who are tired of being pushed around by the Communists." At the same time in a small town in Colorado, a group of men are hard at work running off pamphlets on a small printing press. Their message is simple and direct: "The National Council of Churches aids and abets communism and the National Council of Churches indicts itself on fifty counts of treason against God and Country." They place the pamphlets into pre-addressed mailing envelopes and apply the finishing touch—a rubber stamp imbedded with a hammer and sickle superimposed over the cross of Jesus with the headline: "How Red is the National Council of Churches?"

These are not isolated instances describing the actions of small, uneducated fanatical fringe groups. Included in these organizations are university professors, business executives, newspaper editors, doctors, and lawyers, as well as bricklayers, carpenters, machinists, and clerks. In all, there are one thousand ultraconservative groups with an estimated total membership of 5,500,000, and the number is steadily increasing.

But little do these individuals realize that the cause of the far right holds a terrible irony for them. The irony I refer to is the conscious or unconscious undermining of the very democratic way of life they believe they are fighting to preserve. They fail to recognize that an inherent part of their movement is a basic mistrust in the democratic process and institutions. They are blinded to the consequences of the words of Robert Welch, founder of one of the most powerful anti-Communist leagues, the John Birch Society, when he states that "the John Birch Society will operate under completely authoritative control at all levels. . . ." With these words ringing in our ears let us turn our eyes to the glaring lights of CBS, ABC, and NBC as noted lecturer and author Max Lerner prepares for his press conference at Minneapolis, Minnesota. Mr. Lerner was well aware of the campaign of the far right to prevent his visit, but he was there and so were they with their

"Go Home Lerner" banners. As the press conference began, Mr. Lerner called for the leaders of the group who were unhappy with his visit to come forward and talk things over. Out of the crowd stepped a woman. As Mr. Lerner began to question her, she responded, in angry tone of voice, that she was asking the questions here. Unshaken, Mr. Lerner asked if she had ever read the Bill of Rights. "You're just like all Communists," she answered, "All you want to talk about is the Bill of Rights." Still calm but pressing for an answer, Mr. Lerner, after reminding her that he had spent a lifetime studying this document, once again asked if she had read it. The woman replied in a high-pitched, excited voice: "No, I've never read it, I'm too busy fighting communism."

It is customary for college orators to describe in graphic detail a serious contemporary problem and then with a few bold strokes sketch a simple solution. But this problem is not that easy. For all segments of our society recognize communism as an archenemy of democracy. Thus even well-meaning citizens are susceptible to the call of the "irresponsibles" who replace reason with zeal and disregard means in achieving ends. It is quite clear, then, that punishment or suppression of the extremist is not the answer to the problem. Like the psychotherapist we must help the extremist to regain confidence in the appeal of democracy. In short, we must instill in him a faith in those ideals which have made America strong—ideals which promote trust in the dignity of man. The words of President Kennedy must be repeated again and again: "Let our patriotism be reflected in the creation of confidence rather than crusades of suspicion."

I have seen the results of the "confidence" which President Kennedy so strongly urges us to demonstrate. A few weeks ago a top-ranking member of the American Communist party came to our campus to debate Dr. Charles Layton on the merits of communism. Before he arrived, the far right began to act. Some threatened to cancel their financial pledges to the college; others indicted the administration for providing a foothold for an agent of a foreign power. But the college leaders held firm. What was the result of this encounter between one of communism's ablest spokesmen and a distinguished professor of speech? How foolish and unappealing communism looked to the one thousand people who had assembled on that January night. When it was over the soundly defeated Communist debater turned to his opponent and said: "You were a gentleman, but you hit awfully hard."

This is the product of the confidence that President Kennedy spoke of. So let us remember the power of democracy as epitomized in these words: "You hit awfully hard." Even though the irresponsibles' list of Communists is long and ever growing—Dwight D. Eisenhower; Chief Justice of the Supreme Court Earl Warren; forty-nine leaders of the National Council of Churches; thirty of the ninety-five persons connected with the preparation of the Revised Standard Bible—let us take comfort in the fact that thoughtful people are urging us to maintain a proper historical perspective when viewing the institutions of democracy. Let us remind ourselves of the words of J. Edgar Hoover that all "would do well to recall a recent lesson from history. Both Hitler and Mussolini were against communism. However, it was by what they stood for, not against, that history has judged them."

Analysis

The terse, attention-getting title of this oration focuses directly on the oration's theme and is taken from a phrase used in the fourth paragraph; thus the title fulfills the basic criteria of being brief, relevant, and provocative. The oration itself represents a forthright analysis of a controversial topic, a topic which has worth-while substance and is relevant to the contemporary scene.

Within the broad framework of a problem-solution arrangement, the oration clearly reflects the five-step organizational pattern of contact, justification, thesis, belief, and application. In the introduction, or contact step, three specific instances aid in capturing audience attention and in gaining a sympathetic hearing for the topic. The first three paragraphs, of course, reflect a chronological, time, or "natural" sequence of arrangement. Within the belief or need step, the problem is clearly depicted. In the application step, or conclusion, the speaker focuses on one solution, uses explanation and an example to show it can work, points up the role of the individual, and closes with a quotation which capsules the central theme.

Throughout the oration, numerous specific instances and illustrations are utilized to demonstrate the scope and varied nature of the problem. By implication, these instances are to be viewed as typical of all the examples which could have been cited. In the second, fourth, and twelfth paragraphs, the speaker focuses on his own personal experience with the problem and solution. Expert testimony is used in the form of opinion quotations from John F. Kennedy, J. Edgar Hoover, and William F. Buckley, himself a political conservative. The speaker reasons that although either-or thinking and taking stands more against than for things are characteristic of the political far right, the solution is not to punish or suppress extremists, but to alter their thinking.

The style generally reflects mature, clear, and, at times, impressive language usage. Antithesis is reflected in several phrases, such as "they place the unachievable against the unbearable." Words chosen are normally simple, clear, precise, and yet sometimes vivid.

At least two facets of the oration might have been improved upon. More information about MacLeish, Buckley, and Hoover could have been provided so as to establish more firmly their qualifications to speak on the subject at hand; their opinions thus would have been given more weight. In addition, the speaker could have expanded on the idea that the extremists "replace reason with zeal and disregard means in achieving ends." The idea pinpointed here never was adequately or fully developed, explained, or illustrated.

ONE MAN IN HIS TIME

Carl W. Carmichael, Westminster College

Third Place, 1961 National Finals, Interstate
Oratorical Association Contest

Almost as though it had been taught to hate, my foot
stamped on the little black spider crossing the floor of
my dormitory room. I destroy or run from anything I
fear, and I fear anything I can't understand. I met a
man three summers ago at the mental hospital where I
worked. As he limply climbed onto the soda fountain
stool I could see he had been beaten. His right eye was
blackened and almost closed. His left arm in a sling
seemed to point to the purple welts on his neck and face.
He said, "Nobody understands me," then ordered an ice
cream soda. I gave him the soda but I couldn't tell him
that he was right. Whoever had beaten him didn't
understand him. Men fear that which they don't understand.

We can't understand the insect world because we
can't communicate with it. We can't understand those
mentally ill because we can't communicate with them.
But the problem of communication extends further than
our relationship with insects or even the mentally ill.

Have you ever simply watched people? Only in the
theater of life do we get to be actor and audience.
From day to day we have opportunity to observe many
dramatic situations while we, too, provide the stage

action for those around us. But the theater of life does not always entertain. How often we find the drama to be unpleasant—and yet, how often we ourselves have made the drama unpleasant! Most of the conflicts in this life arise from misunderstanding—the failure of people to communicate with each other. But what is communication? A man speaking? A transference of ideas? Or a complete understanding of attitudes—sincerity, honesty, truth?

William Shakespeare said:

> All the world's a stage,
> And all the men and women merely players.
> They have their exits and their entrances,
> And one man in his time plays many parts.
> . . . the whining schoolboy, with his satchel
> And shining morning face, creeping like snail
> Unwillingly to school.

"Mommy, why can't I go to that school over there? Mommy, today they called me 'nigger.' I don't understand." Benjamin E. Mays, president of Morehouse College in Atlanta, Georgia, in his article entitled "A Plea for Straight Talk Between the Races" said, "The plain truth is that Negroes and white people in the South never had honest communication. Honest communication is built on truth and integrity; and upon respect of the one for the other." Now I ask you, how can we expect children to understand the problems that adults can't even get together and talk about? Without communication there can be no understanding.

Shakespeare's next age is the "soldier, full of strang oaths, and bearded like a pard." "I wonder if

that guy I'm shooting at understands why we're fighting? I wish I did. I'll bet he's just like me in a lot of
ways. But, I'll never know." The Victorian poet
Thomas Hardy wrote these words in his poem "The Man
He Killed":

> I shot him dead because
> Because he was my foe, . . .
> Yes, quaint and curious war is!
> You shoot a fellow down
> You'd treat if met where any bar is,
> Or help to half a crown. . . .

In our world tense situations seek solutions through
violence because of lack of understanding—because of
lack of communication. Would the Cuban people have
remained behind their guns a few weeks ago waiting
for American planes to attack if we had not somehow
failed to communicate that we are peace-loving? Would
the natives of the Congo resist United Nations' aid if
they understood the objectives and true intentions of this
international organization? Conflict does arise from
lack of communication.

Then to another age, "the justice, in fair round
belly . . . full of wise saws and modern instances, and so
he plays his part." Yes, the politician, the leader of the
people on every level of society whose success depends
on his communicative powers. Many people believe that
John Kennedy's most favorable factor during the presi-
dential campaign was the series of debates witnessed by
the public through today's greatest mass communication
medium—television. Through communication we came
to a greater understanding of the motives, desires, and

attitudes of the aspiring politicians, than perhaps in any previous election. They came into our living rooms and we grew to know them personally—understand them— through communication.

Then Shakespeare presents "the lean and slippered pantaloon, with spectacles on nose and pouch on side." We shall consider him the businessman, the man pre- occupied with earning a living, feeding his family, and sometimes suffering from a disease known as misplaced values or gout of the soul. Daily, he communicates with those around him out of necessity. But is he aware of the need for communication and understanding among the parts of the world as well as among the people in his community?

Obviously, from these examples there is a lack of communication in the world today. Men have recog- nized this problem in the past; and have tried to solve it. But all have failed. An international phonetic alphabet was developed. Dr. Zemenhof, a Russian, devised an artificial language known as Esperanto—an interna- tional language devised with the hope that some day all peoples of the world will speak the same language and understand each other. Over one hundred of these artificial languages have been devised. Why weren't they successful? Why won't an international language work? Well, would an international language enable us to communicate ideally with and understand all peoples of the earth? No! You see, it is not the language bar- rier that is hindering our communication in the world today.

BUILDING THE CONTEST ORATION

When Nikita Khrushchev removed his shoe and pounded the table with it at the United Nations this fall, he did not have to speak English or Esperanto or any other language for that matter, to enable anyone to understand him. Mr. Khrushchev was communicating most effectively through his attitude. In striving for peace, I believe the most influential ambassadors this country has had have been in the arts—Leonard Bernstein, Van Cliburn—displaying an attitude of sincerity and dedication to their art. While observing the 1960 winter and summer Olympics over television, I was immensely impressed at the sight of hundreds of athletes representing the nations of the world, competing in the vigorous daily events, cheering for the proud winners, like Wilma Rudolph—with complete disregard for prejudices, socializing in the evenings. Their attitudes were sincere.

The crucial question of our time is—How can the nations and the peoples of the world speak to each other from their minds and from their hearts? An international auxiliary language is not the answer. Politically our main hope today is the United Nations. But I wonder if the political world will ever find the answer. Politically, the nations of the world are all different. But the peoples of these nations are basically the same— the same basic drives—similar likes and dislikes. The success of our academic and cultural exchange programs have indicated this. Van Cliburn was hailed in Russia as a great pianist on a repeat trip just two months ago and today is in the United States expressing himself through the same medium. In the past year Leonard Bernstein received the same enthusiastic welcomes in Russia as the Russian ballet troupe received in America.

If we are to be on peaceful terms with people, we must understand them and we must help them to understand us. We must get together on common ground. This is why our President is instituting a Peace Corps. This is why so many Americans have already volunteered for this project for peace. Communication reflects attitudes. We must first of all be aware—aware of what our attitudes are—aware of the need for honest communication on all levels of society. Second, we must be concerned—not prejudiced, concerned for all peoples. Concerned enough to support foreign exchange programs, and Kennedy's Peace Corps. Third, we must do the communicating—we must take the responsibility and not leave it to the other fellow. In support of the Peace Corps, Hubert Humphrey said, "America's best resource is its people." But, newspaper writer Douglas Welch said, "This is the age of Big Flapping Mouth." What we say and what we do reflects how we feel.

One man in his time plays many parts. You are that man. This is the Time. Whatever part you play, are you communicating understanding through your attitudes? Whether in the world, or in the nation, or in your own home town—understanding must be brought about by communication on the level that all peoples can understand. The success of communication today is dependent on your attitudes.

BUILDING THE CONTEST ORATION

Analysis

The brief, provocative, and relevant title is excerpted from the main quotation in the fourth paragraph and is repeated in the concluding paragraph of the oration for emphasis.

This oration represents a more philosophical handling of the problem-solution speech than "The Irresponsibles"; the problem is important but less controversial. But the speech does reflect the five-step pattern of contact, justification (both combined in the first two paragraphs), thesis, belief, and application.

Various supporting techniques are utilized. A quotation from Shakespeare is skillfully adapted to provide an organizational pattern and topics for some paragraphs. Part of a poem by Thomas Hardy is employed to illustrate a point. In the introduction, or contact step, a factual example rooted in personal experience is used to illustrate the problem; when dealing with the solution, additional factual examples are used. Hypothetical, but probable, illustrations are utilized in depicting the problem. Testimony from Benjamin E. Mays, Hubert Humphrey, and Douglas Welch is employed. When dealing with the solution, the speaker, before presenting his own, shows why some proposed solutions will not work. The speaker then proposes to meet the problem of lack of effective communication with a threefold plan which implements the idea that personal attitude is the key to sound communication. The conclusion, or application step, presents a clear, terse summary emphasis on the main ideas and focuses the responsibility for action on the individual.

The style or language usage is effective. Sentence length is varied; short, hard-hitting sentences are intermingled with longer ones. Skill in narrative description is reflected in the first paragraph. Phrasing and imagery are at times colorful, such as in the image of a "disease known as misplaced values or gout of the soul." Rhetorical questions stimulate and channel the audience's train of thought.

The oration might be strengthened by more fully expanding and illustrating the three facets of the proposed solution. The audience would have a clearer idea of what should be done and how it could be accomplished.

A LIST

Stephen Alan Oxman

First Place, 1963 National Finals, American
Legion High School Oratorical Contest

Man is born with certain unalienable, God-given
rights. Among these rights are the right to live, the right
to have liberty, and the right to pursue happiness. These
rights are the birthright of all men, because they are
men.

But to say that man has the right to life, liberty and
the pursuit of happiness is to say a million things. It
means he has the freedom to speak, the freedom to think,
the freedom to go where he wants, the freedom to laugh,
the freedom to be left alone and so many other freedoms
that it would be impossible to *list* them all.

There was, however, in the latter part of the eighteenth century in America, a group of men who did *list*
some of the basic rights embodied in the Grand Right to
life, liberty and the pursuit of happiness. The *list* that
these men made is perhaps the most important *list* in
history.

When the Constitutional Convention adjourned on
September 17, 1787, there was one criticism repeatedly
advanced at the document which it had produced—it
lacked a bill of rights. This matter had been discussed
on the floor of the convention. In fact, there was a
motion that a committee be formed to draw up a bill of

rights. But when Roger Sherman pointed out that all of the state constitutions already had a bill of rights, the motion was unanimously defeated.

However, when it came time for ratification, the absence of a bill of rights became a focal point in the controversy. The Anti-Federalists argued that since the new national government had a sphere of sovereignty of its own, which affected individuals directly, it should then have a limitation on its unique powers.

To this charge there were two notable replies. The first was offered by James Madison and C. C. Pinckney, among others. They felt that since the new government was one of specific and enumerated powers, it possessed no authority except in those areas where it had been specifically given. They felt that since it was the states who had the residual, plenary powers, it was upon these powers that limitations should be placed. What Madison and Pinckney were saying was this: the Constitution, up until the point where the Bill of Rights begins, says basically what the Federal Government can do. However, at the point where the Bill of Rights starts, it begins to say what the Federal Government *cannot* do.

The second reply was advanced by James Wilson among others. Wilson explained that the Convention had found a bill of rights "not only unnecessary, but impracticable—for who will be bold enough to enumerate all the rights of the people—and when the attempt to enumerate them is made, it must be rememberd that if the enumeration is not complete, everything not expressly mentioned will be presumed to be purposely omitted." [1] Thus Wilson felt that since it is impossible to *list* all the rights of man—and it is, my friends—it would be best not to *list* any.

But these two arguments did not hold, for in the struggle for ratification several states demanded a pledge that once they ratified the Constitution, a bill of rights would be adopted by amendment. And so it was. Within two years after the establishment of the new government, a Bill of Rights was adopted prohibiting Congress to abridge the freedom of religion, of speech, of the press, of assembly, of bearing arms; restricting the Federal Government's authority in quartering troops, in prosecuting citizens for crimes, in inflicting punishments; guaranteeing the citizen a trial by jury in his own district; and the benefits of common law.

So these are the famous rights that we talk so much about. These are the *basic rights* embodied in the Grand Right to life, liberty and the pursuit of happiness. And these are the rights which were put into the Constitution as only a second thought? Yet these are the rights, my friends, which tell the story of mankind. For if you look at all the wars of all the ages, if you look at all the strife between men, you discover a universal cause—one man or group of men has infringed upon the *basic rights* of another man or group of men. It all boils down to that —one man infringing upon the basic rights of another. The inevitable result has been war.

[1] Quoted by Alfred H. Kelly and Winfred A. Harbison, *The American Constitution* (New York: W. W. Norton and Co., 1955), p. 152.

So no one can say that these rights are not important, not after the notorious history which I have just cited. Important?—why they are the lifeblood of humanity. To abuse, neglect or forget them is paramount to inviting self-destruction. All of us in America say we realize this. We realize the all-importance of these rights. But do we? I ask you, "Do we?" when in a recent national Purdue Opinion Poll of high school students regarding their attitudes toward the Bill of Rights

60 per cent thought that books, magazines and newspapers should be censored;

60 per cent saw nothing wrong with the use of third-degree methods by police;

25 per cent believed it right for the government to prohibit people from making speeches;

33 per cent thought that in certain circumstances homes and private persons should be searched without warrant;

33 per cent were unwilling to allow foreigners the same basic freedoms that belong to citizens;

41 per cent would restrict the right to vote.[2]

Just consider these facts and figures, my fellow Americans. Just think about what they mean. They are, to say the least, astonishing. They represent just the kind of foggy, apathetic thinking that is going to get Americans into some very hot water.

[2] National Council for the Social Studies; Civil Liberties Educational Foundation, Inc., *A Program for Improving Bill of Rights Teaching in High School* (New York: Civil Liberties Educational Foundation, Inc., 1962) p. 8, 9.

But let us not be so fast to condemn. How many of us have not felt a little gratified to see the Communist party take setback after setback in the courts of the United States? How many of us do not feel a little more secure when a fellow like the Nazi leader George Rockwell is denied the freedom to speak or hold assembly? But according to the Bill of Rights, every man can speak freely, regardless of how unpopular his views may be. He also has the right to join with others in propagating unpopular views. Now I realize that these rights are not unlimited. I realize that when a person's speech or actions jeopardize either the *basic rights* of others or the security of a nation, that person's exercise of these rights must be limited. But I also realize that this country is founded on a principle of equality. All men are created equal. Oh! but this is the cold war. Everything endangers the national security! Maybe it should be, "All men are created equal *except* Communists and Nazis." But where do we stop? What is to prevent it from becoming "All men are created equal *except* Communists and Nazis and Catholics and Jews and Democrats and Republicans—STOP! When you start qualifying freedom in these ways, when you start qualifying freedom as did the high school students in that opinion poll, when you start *qualifying freedom*—WATCH OUT! for what happens to *you*.

The point I am making, my friends, is this: Man has desired freedom; man desires freedom. He desires the Grand Right to life, liberty and the pursuit of happiness. He desires more especially the *basic rights* embodied in the Bill of Rights of the United States

Constitution. But unfortunately man, over the ages, has desired one more freedom than he can have—he has desired *the freedom not to worry about his freedom*. Today, this freedom can lead only to enslavement. This freedom man cannot have until one great problem has been solved. The problem is *learning how to live together*—yes, together, Russian with American, black with white, man with man. This is the greatest problem man has ever known, for in spite of all the learning of all the ages, man in the twentieth century is still, as he has ever been, responsible for conquest, war and untimely death. Living together. But what does that mean? I will tell you what it means. Living together simply means respecting *the basic rights of others*—respecting the *basic rights*, as embodied in the Bill of Rights of the United States Constitution, of others. Sounds easy, but man has had a very difficult time learning to do it. However, unless man can learn to do it now, in the nuclear age, he may never have another chance.

It is a question of individual responsibility. One individual assuming the responsibility to respect, protect, and cherish not only his *basic rights* but those of his fellow man. Only when this doctrine of *individual responsibility* has been spread far enough and wide enough until it is at the top of men's hearts and minds everywhere, will man have the *freedom not to worry about his freedom*. Only then will it be unnecessary to make a *list* as did our forefathers, for fear that someone would take away their basic rights. And only then, when this doctrine of *individual responsibility* has been spread far enough and wide enough until it is at the top of men's hearts and minds everywhere, will man have solved the greatest problem he has ever known—learning how to live together, yes, together, in kindness, in justice, in mutual respect, in peace, in love—Russian with American, black with white, man with man.

Analysis

This oration represents a straightforward but not sensationalistic approach to an important controversial subject; the speaker has something worth-while to say. The orator accomplishes a difficult task by taking an ideal, the ideal of freedom and basic rights, an ideal that has unique meaning for Americans, and discussing it in a concrete, realistic manner. Freedom is not discussed in vague, generalized terms, but is linked with our happiness and day-to-day living. The central thesis is supported by logic and evidence, undergirded with compelling feeling, and reinforced with simple, clear, dignified language possessing a certain literary flavor.

The problem-solution organization is utilized. The problem of infringements on basic rights, especially the right of free speech, is to be offset by the solution of individual responsibility in respecting the basic rights of others. The theme of basic rights runs throughout the speech, is examined from various perspectives, and gives the oration cohesion.

A meaningful historical context is provided for the Bill of Rights by presenting some of the arguments used both for and against its adoption. The problem of infringement is clarified and made concrete by use of common examples and of a student public opinion poll. Also, the problem is focused directly at the audience and their feelings.

The speaker introduces a novel and insightful idea: One of our basic wants is a desire for the freedom not to worry about our freedom. But the speaker stresses that this want is not satisfied by infringement or restrictions. To increase clarity and meaningfulness, the speaker might have expanded this whole idea more completely.

One characteristic of the style or language usage is the employment of rhetorical questions to stimulate the audience's train of thought. A feeling of vigor and force is gained through use of strong declarative sentences. One particularly effective phrase is the "Grand Right to life, liberty, and the pursuit of happiness."

Several ideas could have been expanded and clarified more fully. What are the specific constitutional and Supreme Court limitations on freedom of speech which traditionally have been accepted by the American people? In addition, the speaker might have been more specific on what the solution of individual responsibility for respecting basic rights involves, especially relative to the free speech problem. Unless a solution is specific and its means of implementation are spelled out, the audience may view it as vague and trite. The causal reasoning in paragraph nine might have been clarified. To say that wars and strife have always been "caused" by infringements on the rights of others is more a description of what usually happened (violation of treaties, border rights, etc.) than a statement of ultimate cause. The real "cause" involves the motivation behind the infringements. Although the speaker's idea may be correct as far as it goes, perhaps the word "cause" is not the most precise one in this context.

THE CONSTITUTION—TEMPLE OF LIBERTY

PATRICIA ANN TURNER

FIRST PLACE, 1962 NATIONAL FINALS, AMERICAN
LEGION HIGH SCHOOL ORATORICAL CONTEST

Once there was a wise old hermit who lived in the hills of West Virginia. He was well known throughout the area for his philosophical insight and profound knowledge. One day some boys from a neighboring village decided to play a trick on the hermit to test his wisdom. They caught a bird and proceeded to the hermit's cave. One of the boys cupped the bird in his hands and called to the hermit. "Say, old man, what is it I have in my hands?" Hearing the chirping and noise, the hermit said it was a bird. "Yes, but is it dead or alive?" asked the boy. If the hermit said the bird was alive, the boy would crush it in his hands. If the hermit said the bird was dead, the boy would open his hands and let the bird fly free. The hermit thought a moment and then replied, "It is what you make it."

As Washington had written to Lafayette, "We now have our freedom, but what are we going to make of it? Any weakness in the Union may ultimately break the band which holds us together."

For a long time the wise members of the Continental Congress had known the truth of the immortal words of Benjamin Franklin, "We must all hang together, or assuredly we shall hang separately." We were suffering from "too little government." There was no central government to deal with the problems of the new country. Finally, after long months of deliberation, our Constitution, our "Temple of Liberty," was fashioned.

Thirty-nine gentlemen in silk stockings, knee breeches, and ruffled shirts signed the documents. One by one, they penned a document to guarantee all the virtues sought by our forefathers—Union, Justice, Tranquillity, Safety, Welfare, and Liberty.

And as they signed, Franklin turned to a friend and pointed to the sun pictured on the back of the chair which had been occupied by the president of the convention. He said, "I have often in the course of the session looked at that sun behind the president without being able to tell whether it was rising or setting. But now at length I have the happiness to know that it is a rising and not a setting sun."

"We the People"—we'll never know in whose brain the idea originated, but we do know that it sounds the heartbeat of the framers of our Constitution. It is the voice of the people, giving expression to their soul's desire—a desire to unite the spirits and hearts of the people "under one roof," in an indestructible Union, making our Liberty forever secure.[1]

In those simple yet powerful words the preamble comes alive with the strong verbs—*Form, establish, insure, provide, promote, secure,* and *ordain.*

"Will it work?" This was the question Franklin asked himself and others of the convention. "It works."

[1] Sol Bloom. *The Story of the Constitution* (Washington, D.C.: United States Constitution Sesquicentennial Commission, 1937) p. 181.

That is the answer 175 years later. It will continue to work as long as "We the People" govern our own country of America.

Thomas Jefferson once said, "The common sense of the common people is the greatest and soundest force on earth." The Founding Fathers of the Constitution had that common sense and forethought when they devised an idea of government so solidly rooted it could grow in power and vision. Its flexibility and adaptability to the requirements of progress have served our every need. It has stood the test of time, war, and depression. Of the people, by the people, for the people, it has preserved, protected, and defended the rights of each and every one.

Yet we take too much for granted this wonderful document of democracy. We naturally think that to which we are accustomed is obvious and needs no justification. We forget the long and painful struggle to achieve our constitutional government. One from which other countries have drawn those elements which could best be adapted to their needs, and now, together with America, are trying to find the way to merge the pattern for a lasting peace. [2]

It has often been said that a man is as tall as heaven when he is free, when he realizes the dignity of his own soul. Yet we often think of freedom as heritage and sometimes acquire a complacent attitude toward our wealth of liberty.

[2] *Ibid.*

When our country was still a line of English colonies along the Atlantic coast, the story is told of a farmer living in New York who tried to tell the people of his native France what life in America was like.

He described the beauty and richness of the land, and the thrilling sight of men and women coming from every country in Europe to be forged together into a new nation. But he talked mostly about freedom. Nothing seemed to amaze him so much as how free a man could be in the New World.

In America, he said, a man is free to work for himself and keep what he earns; he is free from hunger and servitude and abasement; he is free to go to the church he prefers.

The farmer was so afraid his friends in Europe could not comprehend this kind of freedom that he repeated it over and over. [3]

In his book *This American People*, Gerald W. Johnson, says, "What we need is not the flatterer who tells the American citizen what a wonderful fellow he is and what a glorious thing it is to be an American. For the American doctrine, our Constitution, was devised by brave men, for brave men."

Next to the Bible, it is the most precious expression of the human soul—every word offering solace and security, every word a symbol of safety in our life, liberty, and pursuit of happiness. All of its parts are links that bind the people together in an unbreakable chain—a

[3] Jean de Crèvecœur, *Letters from an American Farmer*, quoted by Rewey Belle Inglis in *Adventures in American Literature* (New York: Harcourt, Brace and Co., 1949), p. 777.

chain so beautifully formed that one is reminded of the mystical golden chain which the poet saw binding the earth to God's footstool. [4]

As William E. Gladstone so simply put it, "It is the most wonderful work ever struck off at a given time by the brain and purpose of man."

To the framers, the Constitution was a new Declaration of Independence—a declaration that the hard-won liberty should not perish, but should be made perpetual by pooling our resources and energies in a firm Union. To this end may we constantly give thought and pledge "our lives, our fortunes, and our sacred honor" to that goal, that we might be worthy of those who did so much for us.

In New York Harbor stands a symbol of the liberty and brotherhood which the citizens of a country enjoy under a free form of government. The right hand holds a great torch high in the air, while the left hand grasps a tablet bearing the date of the Declaration of Independence. A broken chain at her feet symbolizes the bonds which chain a people struggling for their freedom. At night the torch in the right hand gleams with light . . . a symbol of liberty shedding light upon the world. [5]

May we ever lift our eyes to that soaring dome where freedom stands, "with her laurel crowned helmet and her grounded shield," and have that one dream in our hearts—the dream that freedom and justice, which

[4] *The Constitution*, You and Your U.S.A. Series (Washington, D.C.: Office of Armed Forces Information and Education, United States Department of Defense).

[5] "Statue of Liberty," *World Book Encyclopedia*, Vol. 10 (Chicago: Field Enterprises, Inc. 1950), p. 4400.

is our heritage, may become that of every nation of the world.

May we always remember the Constitution as our most precious gift. A declaration that liberty and justice shall forever reign—for every man, woman, and child, beneath the Stars and Stripes. Time does not wear down nor eat away its eternal truths. Instead of fading with age, the Constitution takes on new splendor. War does not overturn our "Temple of Liberty," built by our fore-fathers, with a faith which gave them the strength to plan for the ages. With equal faith, may we guard our birthright and hand it down to our posterity as their most precious heirloom—liberty, "the immediate jewel of the soul." [6]

As our President once said, "Ask not what your country can do for you, ask what you can do for your country."

Just as the bird in the cupped hands of the boy, it is in the hands of each American to let our liberty die or make it live.

Analysis

This oration is not problem-solution oriented. Instead, its purpose is to stimulate thought, to depict the nobility of an idea, and to reawaken and deepen feelings toward the Constitution. Such eulogistic speeches too often emerge simply as unbounded, uncritical, oversentimental adulation. Fortunately,

[6] Bloom, *op. cit.*, p. 84.

however, this oration puts praise in its proper perspective by tempering it. The quotation by Gerald W. Johnson in the sixteenth paragraph, the idea that often we take the Constitution for granted, and the idea that the Constitution is "what you make it" all combine to emphasize that all is not perfect and there is room for improvement. The speaker presents a well-rounded analysis of the Constitution's lasting worth and recognizes that it allows for discussion and rectification of weaknesses in it. Constant growth and improvement are stressed and the Constitution is not viewed as static, as perfect for all time.

The oration's basic message, that the value of the Constitution is in our hands, is emphasized by the attention-getting but somewhat trite story in the introduction and again in the concluding paragraph. The oration's title helps create an image basic to the central theme. The oration follows a somewhat loose topical organization. The theme stressed at the beginning and the end of the oration might have been stressed more explicitly throughout.

The speaker employed expert testimony from Americans such as Washington, Franklin, Jefferson, and Kennedy, who were linked with our government. Opinions from others such as Sol Bloom and Gerald Johnson, and from foreign observers, such as Crèvecœur and Gladstone, were also used. The speaker's use of testimony generally was effective, but orators must always avoid overreliance on the opinions of others at the expense of original thinking on their own part. In addition, trite, overused quotations, such as that by Gladstone, usually should be avoided.

The language usage of the speaker is generally clear, correct, appropriate for the subject and occasion, and impressive. The image in the twentieth paragraph of the Statue of Liberty towering in New York Harbor is vivid. Colorful word choice paints effective images. We see "thirty-nine gentlemen in silk stockings, knee breeches and ruffled shirts" and we see that a man is "as tall as heaven when he is free."

A GREAT FUTURE

John M. Mowrer

FIRST PLACE, 1963 NATIONAL FINALS, FUTURE
FARMERS OF AMERICA PUBLIC SPEAKING CONTEST

This is a new age, an age when complete organs of the human body are being replaced with mechanical counterparts, when machines are solving mathematical problems in a few seconds that ten years ago would have taken hours or even days. This is the age when space exploration and satellites are no longer found only in the science fiction book, but are common-day terms. Yes, this is an age when men have both their thoughts and eyes turned skyward.

This, too, is the age when we hear on every hand, that man's oldest existing occupation—agriculture—is fast being shoved aside, that agri-business as a whole is fighting for its very life and has lost its appeal as an employer. Untold numbers of "prophets of doom" are forecasting a dismal future for agri-business. Before we make our decision concerning the future of agriculture let us explore some interesting and revealing facts concerning this American giant. What is it? What has happened to it? and What does the future really hold? In the late 1800's, as the gigantic industrial revolution got a foothold in America and began grinding its way across the countryside, another slower, but no less important revolution was also taking place. This revolution, the agricultural revolution, basically was a change from farming merely as a way of life, to commercial farming, or farming as a business, accomplished by a shift in population from rural to urban areas.

This revolution brought drastic and meaningful changes to the face of America. The changes have continued until now, of the 65 million people employed in the United States, nearly 26 million are employed by agri-business, that industrial giant made up of the producers, processors, distributors, and service personnel for farm products. Nearly 8 million Americans work on farms and ranches, producing food and fiber; another 7 million are engaged in producing for and servicing these 8 million farmers. Eleven million workers process and distribute farm products, and close to half a million scientists are engaged in agri-business work.

When totaled, nearly 40 per cent of existing jobs in America today are in agri-business, jobs vital to the well-being of every American, jobs vital to our country. Agri-business encompasses more than five hundred occupations classified under seven major fields. These general fields include research, industry, education, communication, conservation, agri-service, and farming and ranching.

The last of these categories, farming and ranching, alone is definitely big business, for the farm today requires an average investment of over $43,000. The total assets of farmers is an astounding $200 billion, a figure equal to three fourths the total assets of all the corporations in the United States.

Now, what progress has been and is being made? Is farming standing still? In answer to this question, I quote from a recent report prepared by a governmental committee, which stated that "during the 1950's agricultural productivity increased three times as fast as that of any other industry, and that production per man-hour of labor rose an estimated 90 per cent." Does this sound like a dead or dying industry?

A survey conducted by land grant colleges showed that agri-business needs an estimated 15,000 college graduates each year—but 15,000 aren't available, in fact not even half that number are available. Approximately 7,000 young men and women graduate each year from our agricultural colleges, qualified to fill these 15,000 jobs, so in actuality, there are two futures awaiting the graduate in agri-business.

We can readily see that farming itself is big business, a business vital not only to America's physical well being but of immeasurable importance to our national economy. We must also realize that there are many individuals such as the vocational agriculture teacher, agricultural economist, agriculture insurance agents, agriculture journalists, the soil conservationist, the government regulatory and inspection officers and many more, who owe not only the very birth of their occupations to agriculture, but they depend on the advancement of farming and agri-business for their continuance.

Now let me pose another question. Isn't it true that the number of farms is decreasing and consequently the number of openings in the general field of agri-business are also decreasing? The answer to the above question must be both yes and no, with the emphasis on the no. While the total number of farms has been declining, it is the small, inefficient farms that have been disappearing from the American countryside, while the larger, adequate income farms have actually increased in numbers. For example, in the United States, between 1939 and 1959, there has been a decrease of over 1,800,000 farms with gross incomes below $5,000, while during this same period the number of farms with incomes above $5,000 has increased over one half million. So, it would seem safe to conclude, that while the actual number of openings available in farming, for young men and women interested in farming, has actually declined, the remaining openings are more attractive and will furnish better opportunities for these young men and women. Thus this decline is not as disheartening as it appears on the surface.

As for the answer to the second part of the question, are opportunities declining in agri-business, the answer must be a definite no. The number of openings in agri-business are not declining even though the number of farms is declining. This decline in the number of opportunities in farming has been more than offset by the increase in the number of opportunities in the farm products servicing and processing fields.

We have seen the present and immediate future in agri-business is very promising, but what about the more distant future, when the FFA members of today will be middle-aged? Will the year 2000 be a wonderful year for agriculture? To say for sure, is of course impossible, but we can observe and encourage individuals, groups and ideas which will in our opinion help to make the year 2000 a great one for agriculture. First, by this time, there will be more than 300 million Americans to feed and clothe, with less farmers to raise the products and with less land to do it. Secondly, it would seem probable that Government assistance, both technical and financial will not decrease to any great extent—the fact that America's agriculture progress is the one field where America has far outstripped Russia, lends authority to this supposition.

Thirdly, and most important in my mind, is the fact that our country has an organization such as the FFA which has as its primary purpose "To develop competent, aggressive, rural and agricultural leadership." This statement of purpose holds within its words, a key; a key to the dynamic future of agriculture; a key to the future of agri-business and even more important the key to a Great America.

Yes, agri-business does have a great future, and I intend to be a part of that future.

BIBLIOGRAPHY

I've Found My Future . . . . *in Agriculture,* American Association of Land-Grant Colleges and State Universities, 1958.

Turnbull, Roderick, "The Miracle of Modern Agriculture," Kansas City *Star,* April 21, 1963, Sec. E.

Doerk, R. K. "Importance of Agriculture to Our Nation," *American Vocational Journal, XXXVIII* (May 1963), 20-21.

1960 Census Report.

SELECTED WINNING ORATIONS

Analysis

This oration is not organized as a problem-solution speech. Its goal is to convince the audience that there *is* a great future in agriculture. The organization of the whole oration moves from past to present to immediate future to distant future. The first two paragraphs set the topic of the speech and outline the organizational pattern. In an age of great progress and change, the oration will consider, Is the future of agriculture bleak? The questions What is it? What has happened to it? and What does the future really hold? outline the oration's main topics of agricultural scope, changes, and future. And throughout the speech, rhetorical questions are used as transitional devices to point up organization and begin paragraphs containing new ideas.

The strongest feature of the oration is its excellent employment of statistics for both explanation and proof. Statistics are utilized to describe the scope and nature of agriculture, to illustrate changes, and to prove that a good future for agriculture does exist in the immediate and distant future. The speaker does not simply cite statistics, but, as in paragraphs six, seven, and nine, he interprets them and reasons from them. The speaker seeks to make some statistics meaningful by using round numbers and by comparing them to other figures, as in paragraphs five and seven. In paragraph six, however, the base level or figure from which production per man-hour of labor rose 90 per cent in the 1950's should be specified. The question is, a 90 per cent increase over what?

Expert testimony is used in the form of expert sources who present statistics. To aid in evaluating the qualifications of the source cited, we should know more fully who gathered the statistics and when and how they were collected. We need more specific information concerning the rather vague "government committee report" in paragraph six and the "survey by land grant colleges" in paragraph seven.

BUILDING THE CONTEST ORATION

In the conclusion, in looking to the distant future, while it is good to be specific in stating opinions, the oration would be strengthened if the source behind the first opinion and the evidence behind the second were explicitly provided. An appearance of pure speculation must be avoided when attempting to convince an audience. Wisely, the speaker did tie the role of the Future Farmers of America, the specific audience he was addressing, into the larger picture of the future. The final sentence of the oration tersely restates the thesis which the speaker feels he has proven and contains his personal commitment to that future; by implication, others are urged to make the commitment also.

In his language usage, which was clear and precise, the speaker might have used more action and color words, such as depicting the industrial revolution "grinding its way across the countryside." The term *agri-business* is a good shorthand term which encompasses the many facets of the agricultural industry in addition to farming.

Throughout the oration, the speaker makes his topic seem important and offsets the image of a dying industry by transmitting a sense of dynamic opportunity and challenge.

OPTIMISM

JOSEPH MUNOZ

FIRST PLACE, 1959 FINALS, OPTIMIST INTERNATIONAL
ORATORICAL CONTEST

Please heed to this, my last Will and Testament. I am going to reveal to you a most startling confession.

I am Pessimism, the opposite of Optimism. My life has been completely filled with unhappiness. Never have I been tempted to look at the brighter side of things. I have influenced many people to follow me. Those under my influence have been like refugees clutched in the grips of communism, not knowing what the true meaning of America really is. My soul has been filled with so many black spots that I am pleading forgiveness from God and from you, because each spot represents misery, loss of integrity, and moral blight in the human family. I remember clearly, but sadly and ashamed, when I, Pessimism, reigned supreme. Over the centuries I have had my periods of great influence— the dark ages, times of aggression. But it was after the Second World War that I was most influential. I had cast a dark shadow on many innocent people, making them become less and less optimistic. It was believed that people of differing creeds, ideals, and culture could not coexist peaceably in this world. Yes, Fears, Hatreds, Tensions, and Violence are my legacy to man.

It is true, I have been wrong about Optimism. Optimism, the very antithesis of my way of life, is my bitterest enemy. And what battles were waged for the proponents of that hated attitude. But now I have begun to realize the necessity for Optimism. Men such as Einstein and Edison succeeded because they were optimistic. Think of the many drawbacks that faced them. They undoubtedly did the same experiment over hundreds of times, until finally each was successful. Though I nagged and tempted them, they paid no heed to me, and it is men like these who will lead the way to happiness.

As today we recognize the necessity to isolate a deadly, infectious disease, so must we isolate attitudes and ideas like mine. Without optimism, what would this world be like? Pessimism can produce nothing but a spherical mass of dreary, ignorant, miserable people. But so long as there are optimistic people in this world, we are assured that there will always be smiles. So Optimism is, in part, a "ray of light in a dark world." Optimism has a radiant contagion all its own wherever it is, in whatever situation it confronts. And, of a reverse nature is Pessimism in its own limiting, debilitating way.

I am reminded of a person who was very optimistic. He was a baseball coach who managed the worst team in the city. Their next game was to be played against the best team in the city. When interviewed he was asked what he thought the results of the game would be. He replied, "It's going to be a tough game, but we're going to win it." Yes, he was optimistic. If it had been another coach under my influence he would have probably replied, "We ain't got a chance." Optimism is not only good for a person's health, but also, as in the case of the coach, it denotes confidence and its attendant spurt of pep and energy. You may ask, "How does a pessimistic person become optimistic after being clutched in the talons of Pessimism for such a long time?" This, I have learned, and this is my advice to you: God created all, so there is good in all.

It is my sincere hope that my confession may not be arriving too late to serve as a guidepost for others who may be heading in the wrong direction. It is known that the baleful influence of pessimism is slowly dying, but that it will not be completely eradicated until every living person realizes its degenerating influence and weeds it out, never to return.

> If you think you're beaten you are;
> If you'd like to win, but don't think you can,
> It's almost a cinch you won't.
> Think big and your deeds will grow,
> Think small and you'll fall behind,
> Life's battles don't always go
> To the stronger or faster man
> But sooner or later, the man who wins is the
>   fellow who thinks he can.

With these thoughts I sign and seal my testament, this 19th day of April, 1959.

Analysis

The purpose of this oration is to reawaken interest in and reenergize devotion to the spirit of optimism. The use of the first-person narrative form throughout the oration promotes audience interest and a sense of personal intimacy. Attention and interest also are promoted in other ways. The opening two sentences catch attention and create suspense. The elements of revelation and confession stimulate interest. Emphasis on the conflict between optimism and pessimism arouses attention.

In paragraphs three and five, good examples of the effects of optimism are presented. A similar detailed illustration of the undesirable effects of pessimism might have been presented to complete the contrast.

Probably paragraphs three and four should have been reversed in order; then the first part of the oration would emphasize pessimism and the two examples of optimism would come in adjacent paragraphs. The verses at the conclusion of the oration reinforce the central idea concerning the force of optimism. However, although the final sentence of the oration is appropriate to the form of the oration, it is anticlimactic in tone and emphasis to the oration's thesis.

Simple, clear, yet forceful language generally was utilized. Common language with meaning is seen in such phrases as "spirit of pep and energy," but such widely used phrases sometimes may seem trite. Forceful and vivid language is reflected in the following phrases: "My soul has been filled with so many black spots"; "fears, hatreds, tensions and violence"; "a spherical mass of dreary, ignorant, miserable people."

However, the idea that "God created all, so there is good in all" should have been explained and illustrated more fully; it seems too vague and general.

WHAT FREEDOM MEANS TO ME

Janice Woelfle

First Place, 1961-1962 National Finals, Veterans of
Foreign Wars "Voice of Democracy" Contest

Three Americans were out sightseeing in a Soviet
city two years ago. One was Senator Henry M. Jackson,
the second was a U.S. Army officer, and the third a Rus-
sian-speaking official of the U.S. Embassy. It was a
unique day for them. In their tour of the U.S.S.R.,
they'd managed for once to shake off their Kremlin-ap-
pointed guide.

As they walked down the street, a young man suddenly accosted them. He was about thirty years old,
quite well-dressed for a Russian, with the look of a
professional person.

"Are you Englishmen?" the young man said in
Russian.

The Embassy man replied: "No, we're Americans."

"Americans! That's even better," the young man
said excitedly. "I've wanted so long to talk to an
American."

"Why?" the Embassy man asked.

"Because you Americans are such lucky people.
You can read what you want, hear what you want, say
what you want. We can't."

The young man peered nervously over his shoulder
to see if anyone was listening. He knew he was risking

his life to speak like that. "Always remember," he went on, "*they* aren't fooling us about you Americans. We want this to be your kind of world." Then he walked away. Fast.[1]

This incident, experienced and related by Senator Henry M. Jackson, is typical of the effect democracy has on the people of the world; and it is *so* true. We *are* lucky!

Because of democracy, we can go to a public library and select any book from the *Iliad* or the *Odyssey*, to *Alice in Wonderland*. We can listen to the Classical Hour, the Top Fifty Tunes, Back to the Bible broadcast, or political panels on our radios without fear of being found and punished. We, young and old alike, have the unequaled privilege of casting our vote for class officers, school cheerleaders, or the President of the United States.

I am seventeen years old and a senior in high school. Next year, I plan to go on to college and eventually I hope to become a teacher. I have been free to make my vocational and college choice. My family attends church together each Sunday, and we are free to choose our own church. Every year we take a vacation and are free to enjoy the tumbled splendor of the Rockies, the wild coast of Maine, or the warm, sunny beaches of California without having to apply for a passport or ask for permission.

[1] An encounter described by Senator Jackson in "The Man in the Street," included in the book *The Day I Was Proudest to Be an American*, edited by Donald B. Robinson (Garden City, N.Y.: Doubleday & Co., 1958).

My father is president of his local electrical union where they are free to bargain for higher wages or improved working conditions. I can choose between a movie or a football game; my family can purchase all types of clothes from Bermuda shorts to the most beautiful of formals.

Freedom of press, freedom of religion, freedom of speech, freedom of choice, the right to vote—*all* freedoms are made possible only through democracy.

Yes, democracy is voting in November, going to the church of our choice, speaking for what we feel is right, and being able to decide what we will read, see, hear, and do. But it is more than this. It is also the shout of a crowd as their team makes the final touchdown; it's the glow in the eyes of a little girl as she sits on Santa's knee; it's the joy on a three-year-old's face as he pretends that he's a boat in a mud puddle. It is the tender look on a mother's face as she gazes at her new-born child. She knows his future is insured because he was born in a free, democratic country.

Countless times throughout our history we have defended our rights and the rights of other people to be free, but the job is far from done. To further protect and insure the future of every baby, now and yet to come, we must continuously speak for democracy. Yes, we must *act* for democracy. For only through our democratic processes come the guarantees of rights, liberty, and freedom. Our freedom is a give-and-take process, a mutual agreement among Americans to "pursue happiness" as long as it doesn't infringe on the rights of others.

Yes, our country *is* a great country and it presents a great hope to the Communist-held world.

"Always remember," the young Russian continued, "*they* aren't fooling us about you Americans. We want this to be your kind of world."

Freedom is our heritage. Freedom is our opportunity. Freedom is our *job*.

ANALYSIS

This oration aims at inspiring, at reenergizing already existing beliefs. It seeks to ennoble the concepts of freedom and democracy and to achieve our rededication to them.

Although the subject and perhaps even the title of the oration may be determined by the rules of the contest, the method of handling the subject, the real opportunity for creativity, remains in the hands of the speaker. The rules of this scriptwriting contest specify the delivery of a speech as a radio speech via a real or simulated broadcast medium. But in comparison with speeches in most high school oratory contests, the only real difference here is the absence of visual delivery, of gestures and body movement. In this contest, matters of sound content, creativity, organization, language, and vocal delivery remain extremely vital. Because visual delivery is lacking, however, the speaker must be sure that clarity, enthusiasm, preciseness, sincerity, and so forth, are conveyed even more fully through use of language and vocal delivery.

Audience attention and interest initially are gained in this oration through the use of an extended dramatic narrative which leads up to the central thesis: Americans are fortunate to possess freedom and democracy. However, the story is perhaps a little too long in proportion to the total length of the speech.

The speaker widely employs specific examples of the varied facets of life in a democracy; she seeks to define democracy through examples. Some of the examples are general ones common to most Americans. Other examples relate to the speaker herself, to her father, or to her family.

The speaker's clear, simple yet forceful language usage is sometimes picturesque: "The joy on a three-year-old's face as he pretends that he's a boat in a mud puddle."

The final four paragraphs constitute the conclusion, or application step, and here the speaker appeals to patriotic values and motives, calls for action, and seeks rededication. The basic idea contained in the oration's opening story is again referred to and the final paragraph achieves emphasis through use of parallel structure.

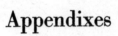

Appendixes

APPENDIX A

BUILDING THE EXTEMPORANEOUS SPEECH

Oratory, debate, and extempore speaking are three standard events featuring original speech which are of long standing in educational forensics. Oratory was first to come on the scene, followed by debate, then the extemporaneous speech. Of the three events, less has been written about the extempore speaking contest than about the other two. Perhaps there is less one can say about it, yet the principles underlying the extemporaneous speech have much in common with most of the public speaking we find in life's situations. Many of the ideas concerning content, forms of support, delivery, organization, and language presented previously also apply to the extemporaneous speech. In this brief appendix, we propose to consider three major aspects of the event: one, the nature and character of extemporaneous speech; two, rules and regulations which govern the mechanics of the event; three, suggestions for being a proficient and effective competitor.

I

The extempore speech should not be confused with impromptu speaking, which is speaking on the spur of the moment without previous thought or planning. The extemporaneous speech requires both general and particular preparation. Neither should the event be likened to oratory. The oration is memorized; the extempore speech is not. The oration stands as a set piece of creative writing, characterized by imagery of language, emotionalized ideas, strong motivational appeals, and a delivery marked by dramatic and personal elements. It may be delivered almost verbatim again and again; but the extempore speech is usually delivered only once, and if it is delivered more than once on the same subject it should vary

189

in manner of language and the way ideas are managed. An oration is more a work of art than the extempore speech. The orator paints portraits of ideas; the extempore speaker gives a snapshot view of them. The extempore speaker, in some ways, has more in common with the debater than the orator. He must be ready to adjust himself speedily to many factors which are unpredictable. The point is, the orator has weeks to put his ideas into shape and properly phrase them, while the extemporaneous speaker has only a few minutes. Obviously, the extempore speaker must be of agile mind and able to control his personal resources under pressure. He must think quickly and adjust himself to his subject and occasion.

As we think of debate, oratory, and extempore speech, it should be clear that the authors' purpose is not to reason why one is more worthy as an educational experience than another. Each has its individual merits and educational values. Ideally speaking, a student should have experience in all three areas. Probably the extempore speech contest is least demanding upon the student's time and effort; however, it offers a unique and peculiar challenge for the courageous bright student who will profit by the experience of formulating his thoughts for a definite purpose on a definite topic in a short period of time. There are many students who could make a creditable showing in debate or oratory by sheer dogged determination and perseverance, but there are relatively few who can adequately rise to the occasion demanded by the extemporaneous speech. This puts a premium upon personal maturity, qualities of leadership, creative imagination and spontaneity in oral communication. Thus, it stands as an excellent training device for personal growth and general improvement in speaking ability.

The extemporaneous speaker must deal with the element of chance, particularly when it comes to drawing his topic. While this may be a limitation on the one hand, acting as a handicap for the would-be winner, it has positive merit on the other hand for it teaches a young person to cope with the element of chance, a common factor in everyday life. To do well with a poor topic may do more toward building strength of character than the ability to do well with an excellent topic.

II

The rules and regulations governing the mechanics of the event may vary somewhat from state to state and from contest to contest within the state. The Kansas State High School Activities Association, for example, in outlining the ground rules for the 1963-1964 extemporaneous speech at festival events, includes the following essentials:

1. There should be one general subject for the extempore speech, selected and approved each year by a special forensic committee and the executive board. The topic for 1964 is "Domestic Affairs as They Concern the Nation." Twenty-five subtopics will be selected from four leading periodicals covering the months of December 1963 and January and February of 1964. The magazines are *Time, Newsweek, U.S. News & World Report,* and the *American Observer.*

2. The contestant draws three subtopics, chooses one, and returns the other two. After drawing his topic, he has thirty minutes to prepare his speech by himself without help from his coach or other persons. He is free to consult any printed matter he may bring with him. He may use notes, but they must be confined to a single three-by-five-inch card.

3. The speech should not be less than five nor longer than seven minutes in length.

4. The speaker will be given an over-all rating: I—Excellent, II—Very good, III—Average, IV—Below Average.

5. The judges are instructed to consider five major factors which are not weighted equally. Their relative importance as bearing upon the combined total effectiveness of the speech is determined by each individual judge. The five factors are (a) adherence to the subject; (b) information, grasp of the materials as applied to developing his ideas; (c) organization,

arrangement and sequence of ideas with appropriate introduction and conclusion; (d) diction, use of appropriate language, pronunciation and enunciation of words; (e) delivery, a direct, animated, communicative manner and skill in the use of note cards.

The pattern of rules and regulations as described above is in general a conventional one and is similar to the procedure used in most states.

III

1. *Preparation.* There are two stages of preparation: general preparation, which takes place weeks and months before the contest, and specific preparation, at the time of the event. The preparation which counts the most is reading, thinking, and observation long before the time of the contest. It is important that you build a reservoir of knowledge and information in advance. Read extensively in the subject areas from which the specific topics may be drawn. Make written and mental notes of the more vital and controversial matters and discuss them with your teachers and other students. Develop original ideas of your own about current developments concerning national domestic affairs. Insight into your subject is the key to the whole event. It will help you speak to the point, it will help you in organizing your materials, and it will be a fundamental source for your self-assurance. There is no substitute for adequate background and information.

2. *Choosing your subject.* Usually it is best to select a topic about which you know the most, but this is not the only criterion. Favor a topic which lends itself advantageously to a breakdown into classified subtopics. Favor a topic about which you can be specific in using facts and names, and in citing cases. Moreover, take into consideration a subject about which you can be original and speak with some personal enthusiasm and conviction and develop a strong motivational appeal. When possible, select a subject from which audience and judges can

gain some new knowledge and insights and one which enables you to make a unique interpretation and draw some original conclusions. Always favor a topic which lends itself to specific and concrete treatment. Avoid vague, general, abstract treatment of your speech materials.

3. *Developing your chosen topic.* After you have your topic, your first step is to settle upon your central purpose. Fix your target clearly in your mind. This will guide you in planning and arranging your ideas in a sequence that makes sense. The topics from which you may choose usually permit you to make one of two general approaches: (a) an analytical discussion in which there are elements of information, exploration, and interpretation; (b) straight, direct argumentation in which you take a definite stand for or against a proposal, winding up your speech with a recommendation and a forceful appeal for some form of action. In the first approach, you deal with value judgements and insights which help your listener to understand more clearly what you are talking about, while in the second approach you deal directly with a question of policy involving some form of action. Usually straight argument dealing with a policy is easier to handle and is more suitable for organization; however, a combination of a sound, penetrating analysis out of which a clean-cut policy is developed can be very effective. This approach leaves more room for originality and usually deals with substance which is thought-provoking and in some instances may have a strong motivation appeal.

The following steps may be useful in planning and organizing your talk: (a) Formulate in your mind the point of view you wish to stress in your speech. Get your central purpose and idea clearly before you and figure out roughly just how you wish to state your central thesis. Be sure you have a clear-cut central idea and that you state it clearly and stick to it. (b) Quickly get to work and block out the main points or headings you want to use in support of the central thesis, then work in facts, reasons, examples, authorities for supporting and developing the main points. This is the heart of your speech and should use about two thirds to three fourths of your speaking time. (c) Make your application, conclusion, or plan of action. In other words, capitalize on the need picture you have created. (d) Now turn your thoughts to the introduction and opening remarks. Don't let this final step throw you off balance. You build your house before you design and build the porch. Don't be too concerned about the use of spectacular attention devices, but be more concerned about creating an impression of the importance of your subject and preparing the minds of the judges for a clear understanding of what you plan to say. The introductory phase should always be brief. (e) Having finished your fourth and final step, quickly scan the key points of your entire speech to get a clear, unified thought picture in mind. If you have time, go over your speech in your own mind or say it rapidly in an undertone from beginning to end before going to the platform.

4. *Additional Suggestions.* (1) Aim to complete your speech before the timekeeper cuts you off. To be cut off spoils the unified effect of your speech. One of the most consistent prize-winning students of this event we have known made it a rule to stop one minute before his time was up. (2) Use your best points early in your speech. In a short speech of only five or six minutes, you must come to grips with the crux of the matter before you reach the half-way point. Don't save the best for the last for you may never be able to give your choice points before the timekeeper cuts you off. Make a good impression upon the judges early in your speech. Do this and you have a psychological advantage. If you start off making a poor impression during the first half of your allotted time, it is doubtful if you can do much to pull the speech out of the fire and save the situation during the latter half. (3) When possible, use the compartment or catalog method in arranging and listing your points, in the one-two-three manner. Never use more than four points—two or three would be better. Some very successful coaches make it a rule never to use more than

two points. (4) When delivering your speech, make what you say sound important. Avoid the casual, indifferent, I-don't-care attitude. (5) Make your ending decisive, short, and crisp. Never close your speech as though you were stringing it out just to fill in the time you have left. Close with a definite, positive punch. (6) Remember this is not a popularity contest; therefore, don't try to throw your weight around to impress the judges with your humor or your cleverness or what a jolly good fellow you are.

APPENDIX B

SELECTED SOURCES ON THE AMERICAN CONSTITUTION

Barnes, William R. (ed.) *The Constitution of the United States.* New York: Barnes and Noble, 1956. (Paperback)

Beard, Charles A. *An Economic Interpretation of the Constitution.* New York: Macmillan Co., 1935. (Paperback)

Bloom, Sol. *The Story of the Constitution.* Washington, D.C.: United States Constitution Sesquicentennial Commission, 1937.

Brown, Robert E. *Charles Beard and the Constitution: A Critical Analysis of "An Economic Interpretation of the Constitution."* Princeton, N.J.: Princeton University Press, 1956.

Corwin, Edward S. *The Constitution and What It Means Today.* New York: Atheneum Publishers, 1963. (Paperback)

Douglas, William O. *A Living Bill of Rights.* Garden City, N.Y.: Doubleday & Co., 1961.

Dumbauld, Edward. *The Bill of Rights and What It Means Today.* Norman, Okla.: University of Oklahoma Press, 1957.

Farrand, Max. *The Fathers of the Constitution.* New Haven, Conn.: Yale University Press, 1921.

Farrand, Max. *The Framing of the Constitution of the United States.* New Haven, Conn.: Yale University Press, 1913. (Paperback)

Farrand, Max (ed.). *Records of the Federal Convention of 1787.* 4 vols. Rev. ed. New Haven, Conn.: Yale University Press, 1937.

The Federalist: A Commentary on the Constitution of the United States, by Alexander Hamilton, James Madison, and John Jay, ed. Roy P. Fairfield. Garden City, N.Y.: Doubleday & Co., 1961. (Paperback)

SOURCES ON THE AMERICAN CONSTITUTION

Hand, Learned. *The Bill of Rights.* New York: Atheneum Publishers, 1964. (Paperback)

Jones, Putnam F. (ed.). *The Constitution of the United States: 1787-1962.* Pittsburgh: University of Pittsburgh Press, 1963.

Madison, James. *Journal of the Federal Convention,* ed. E. H. Scott. Chicago: Scott, Foresman & Co., 1893.

Orfield, Lester B. *The Amending of the Federal Constitution.* Ann Arbor, Mich.: University of Michigan Press, 1942.

Pritchett, C. Herman. *The American Constitution.* New York: McGraw-Hill Co., 1959.

Read, Conyers (ed.). *The Constitution Reconsidered.* New York: Columbia University Press, 1938.

Rickard, John A., and McCrocklin, James H. *Our National Constitution.* 2d ed. Harrisburg, Pa.: Stackpole Co., 1957.

Schuyler, Robert Livingston. *The Constitution of the United States: An Historical Survey of Its Formation.* New York: Macmillan Co., 1923.

Van Doren, Carl. *The Great Rehearsal: The Story of the Making and Ratifying of the Constitution of the United States.* New York: Viking Press, 1948. (Paperback)

Warren, Charles. *The Making of the Constitution.* Boston: Little, Brown & Co., 1928.

Weinberger, Andrew D. *Freedom and Protection: The Bill of Rights.* San Francisco: Chandler Publishing Co., 1962. (Paperback)

Index

INDEX

3464